Nancy Clark's Food Guide for New Runners

Nancy Clark's Food Guide for New Runners

Getting It Right the First Time

Meyer & Meyer Sport

British Library Cataloguing in Publication Data
A catalogue record for this book is available from the British Library

Nancy Clark's Food Guide for New Runners
Maidenhead: Meyer & Meyer Sport (UK) Ltd., 2009
ISBN: 978-1-84126-262-8

© 2009 by Meyer & Meyer Sport (UK) Ltd.
Aachen, Adelaide, Auckland, Budapest, Cape Town, Graz, Indianapolis,
Maidenhead, New York, Olten (CH), Singapore, Toronto
 Member of the World
Sports Publishers' Association (WSPA)
www.w-s-p-a.org

Printed and bound by: B.O.S.S Druck und Medien GmbH, Germany
ISBN: 978-1-84126-262-8
E-Mail: info@m-m-sports.com
www.m-m-sports.com

Contents

Section I. Day-to-Day Eating—The Right Way

Section II. Carbs, Protein, Fats and Fluids—The Right Balance

Section III. Sports Nutrition—The Right Foods at the Right Time

Section IV. Weight and Runners—The Right Diet

Acknowledgements

With sincere thanks and appreciation to:

Hans Jürgen Meyer and Thomas Stengel for their publishing help.

Andrea Eisen for the design work that nourishes the eyes.

Larry Armstrong, PhD for granting permission to use the Urine Color Chart.

My husband, John McGrath, and children, John Michael and Mary, for giving balance to my life, and nourishing me with their love.

My clients, many of whom are new runners, for sharing their experiences and teaching me how to better help others with similar questions and concerns. I love your enthusiasm!

Dedication

I dedicate this book to the new runners who have the courage and spirit to embark on a new sport that will not only enhance their health but also add pleasure and pride to their lives.

May this information help these everyday champions enjoy high energy, good health and "smooth running" both in life and on the roads.

Nancy Clark, MS, RD, CSSD

Certified Specialist in Sports Dietetics
Healthworks Fitness Center, Chestnut Hill, MA

www.nancyclarkrd.com

Foreword

People start running for many reasons:

"I recently graduated from college and had an active lifestyle. I'm now sitting behind a desk from 9:00 to 5:00, and I hate being so sedentary," reports Patrick, a 24-year-old computer programmer. He decided to take up running to help him maintain a desirable weight and fitness level. Plus, he eventually wanted to be able to run the Boston Marathon.

"I want to lose weight, so I've started running. My eating has been pathetic for many years, and it's time to get on a better path toward better health and higher energy," admitted Caroline, a 54-year-old teacher and aspiring runner. She felt good about taking steps to live a more active lifestyle. She'd seen her parents become overweight, underfit and unhealthy, and she didn't want to travel the same path. Nor did she want her failing health to become a burden to her children.

"I've recently retired and I finally have time to invest in myself. I've always wanted to run, but I never managed to make the time nor find the energy to do so," claimed Susan, a former international sales manager and current grandmother. She wanted to be able to not only keep up with her grandchildren but also preserve her good health for the long run.

"I'm starting to run as a part of my goal to raise money for the Leukemia and Lymphoma Society's Team in Training. I lost a dear friend to leukemia, and this is how I want to honor him," said David. He had learned about the millions of dollars raised by charity runners and he felt inspired to dedicate himself to this worthy cause – as well as to enjoy a new adventure, new friends, and a healthier lifestyle.

Clearly, people start running for many reasons. You, too, likely have your own personal goals for performance, health and weight – and enjoyment of what running can add to your life. You also know that eating wisely will help you better accomplish your goals. So how can you best fuel your body to run for 10 minutes, 10 miles, 10 years or whatever your goals may be? In *Nancy Clark's Food Guide for New Runners: Getting It Right the First Time*, you'll find answers to your questions about:

- What to eat before you run, so you have energy to enjoy each training session.

- What to eat after a hard run, to help you refuel and recover.

- How to lose undesired body fat while maintaining energy to train.

- Which sports drinks, gels, energy bars and other engineered foods can help you reach your goals.

- The best foods to fuel your body and also invest in good health and longevity.

Because the combination of running and good nutrition is incredibly powerful, you do, indeed, want to "get it right the first time" by establishing sustainable ways to eat that will contribute to life-long enjoyment of running. In this *Food Guide for New Runners*, you'll come to appreciate that food is not only fuel, but also more powerful than medicine. And equally important, food is one of life's pleasures!

Fuel wisely, eat well and enjoy a satisfying running experience.

Nancy Clark, MS, RD, CSSD
Board Certified Specialist in Sports Dietetics
Healthworks Fitness Center
1300 Boylston Street
Brookline, MA 02467

www.nancyclarkrd.com

SECTION I

DAY-TO-DAY EATING —THE RIGHT WAY

Chapter 1
Daily Eating for Health and High Energy

Food is not only one of life's pleasures; it is also a powerful performance enhancer. As a new runner, you will soon come to appreciate that food can help you train at your best so you can enjoy miles of smiles, to say nothing of good health and future well-being. Fueling yourself well on a daily basis requires time-management skills. That is, you need to find time to food shop, so you'll have wholesome sports foods available. You also need to find time to fuel up and refuel on a schedule that enhances your energy and improves your performance.

In this chapter, I'll share with you the basic tips about how to eat well, even when you are eating on the run. But first, it helps to understand my definition of "eating well." My simple definition is to eat:

Some Top Sports Foods

The following top sports foods offer mainly cook-free and convenient best bets for people who eat and run.

Some of the best fruits for vitamins A and/or C:
oranges, grapefruit, cantaloupe, strawberries, kiwi, mango

Some of the best vegetables for vitamins A and/or C:
broccoli, spinach, green and red peppers, tomatoes, carrots, sweet potato, winter squash

The easiest sources of calcium for strong bones:
Low-fat milk, yogurt, cheese, calcium-fortified orange juice, soy milk and tofu

Convenient cook-free proteins for building and protecting muscles:
Deli roast beef, ham, and turkey, canned tuna and salmon, hummus, peanut butter, tofu, cottage cheese

Cook-free grains for carbohydrates and fiber:
High-fiber breakfast cereals (preferably iron-enriched), wholesome breads and bagels, whole-grain crackers

1. Three kinds of food at each meal.

2. Two kinds of food at each snack.

3. Evenly sized meals every four hours throughout the day (not "crescendo eating" with a small breakfast and a large meal at the end of the day).

4. At least 90% of the calories from quality foods and, if desired, the remaining 10% from sweets and treats.

Luckily for most of today's runners, you don't have to be a good cook to eat well. You can still manage to optimally nourish your body even if you are eating on the run and spending little time in the kitchen.

Here are some guidelines to help you make optimal food choices:

- Try to eat at least two cups of fruit and 2 $\frac{1}{2}$ cups of vegetables per day

- Choose a variety of colors of fruits and vegetables each day: red apples, green peppers, orange carrots, white potatoes…

- Enjoy whole-grain products at least two times per day, such as oatmeal for breakfast and whole wheat bread for lunch. If desired, the rest of the recommended grains can come from enriched grain products, such as enriched pasta. In general, at least half the grains should come from whole grains. (Whole grains include whole wheat, rice, oats, corn and barley.)

- Drink 3 cups (24 ounces/ 720 ml) each day of fat-free or low-fat milk or yogurt, or eat the calcium-equivalent in low-fat cheese (1.5 ounces/ 45 g of cheese = 8 ounces/ 240 ml of milk or yogurt).

- When selecting and preparing meat, poultry, dry beans, and milk or milk products, make choices that are lean, low-fat or fat-free.

- Limit your intake of saturated and trans fats and choose healthier oils such as olive and canola oils, nuts and nut butters, and oily fish such as salmon.

Dietary Recommendations for Good Health

By following these dietary recommendations, you can substantially reduce your risk of developing heart disease and other diseases of aging.

- Balance calorie intake and physical activity to achieve and maintain a healthy body weight.
- Consume a diet rich in vegetables and fruits.
- Choose whole-grain, high-fiber foods.
- Consume fish, especially oily fish, at least twice a week.
- Limit your intake of saturated fat to <7% of energy, trans fat to <1% of energy, and cholesterol to <300 mg per day by:
  —choosing lean meats and vegetable alternatives.
  —selecting fat-free (skim), 1%-fat, and low-fat dairy products.
  —minimizing intake of partially hydrogenated fats.
- Minimize your intake of beverages and foods with added sugars.
- Choose and prepare foods with little or no salt.
- If you consume alcohol, do so in moderation.
- When you eat food that is prepared outside of the home, follow these dietary recommendations.

Source: Diet and Lifestyle Recommendation Revision 2006: A Scientific Statement From the American Heart Association Nutrition Committee. A. Lichtenstein et al. Circulation 2006; 114:82-96.

"It's so simple most people miss it. 'Eat to run.'
I eat with a purpose: I use food for fuel. This helps me pick the right foods so I can perform better."

Kenny Baldo, Matawan, NJ

Balancing Your Diet

Food can be divided into four groups: grain, fruit & vegetable, dairy and protein. The trick to balancing the recommended servings of foods during your day is to plan to have at least three out of four food groups per meal, and one or two food groups per snack, such as:

	Breakfast	Lunch	Snack	Dinner	Snack
1. Grain	Bran flakes	bread		spaghetti	popcorn
2. Fruit & Vegetable	banana	apple baby carrots	berries	tomato sauce	cider
3. Dairy	milk		yogurt	Parmesan cheese	
4. Protein	almonds	tuna fish		ground turkey	

Carbohydrates for Your Sports Diet

By eating grains, fruits and vegetables as the foundation of each meal, you'll consume about 55 to 65 percent of your calories from carbohydrates. This is exactly what you need for a high-energy sports diet. These carbohydrates are stored in muscles in the form of glycogen and provide the energy you need for running.

Grain foods are a popular source of carbohydrates for most active people. Some new runners believe they will get fat if they eat breads, cereals and pastas at each meal. False. Carbohydrates are not fattening; excess calories are fattening. (See Chapter 14: Weight Reduction for Runners.)

Fruits and vegetables are also excellent sources of carbohydrates. But some runners have trouble figuring out how to consume daily the recommended two cups (500 g) of fruits and 2 $\frac{1}{2}$ cups (600 g) of vegetables. As one new runner sheepishly remarked, "I'm lucky if I eat that much in a week." The trick is to eat large portions. Most runners can easily enjoy a banana (which counts as 1 cup of fruit) and 8 ounces (1 cup/ 240 ml) of orange juice in the morning. That's the minimal two cups of fruit for the day! A big bowl of salad filled with colorful tomato, carrot and pepper can account for the minimal recommended 2 $\frac{1}{2}$ cups of vegetables.

Fruits: Recommended Daily Intake—2 or more cups (500+ g)

Here's what counts as "one cup":

Orange Juice	8 ounces	240 ml
Apple	1 small	100 g
Banana	1 small	100 g
Canned Fruit	1 cup	240 g
Dried fruit	$\frac{1}{2}$ cup	80 g

Vegetables: Recommended Daily Intake—2 $\frac{1}{2}$ to 3+ cups (600 to 700+ g)

Here's what counts as "one cup":

Broccoli	1 medium stalk	200 g
Spinach	2 cups raw	60 g
Salad Bar	1 average bowl	100 g
Spaghetti Sauce	1 cup	250 g

Fruits and vegetables are truly nature's vitamin pills, chock full of vitamin C (to help with healing), beta-carotene (to protect against cancer), fiber (to aid with regular bowel movements) and numerous other vitamins and minerals. The following pages offer suggestions for simple ways to boost your veggie intake.

Eat More Veggies!

If you struggle to consume the recommended two to three servings of vegetables per day, the following tips may help you to enhance your vegetable intake—and your health.

- Eat more of the best vegetables, less of the rest. In general, dark green, deep yellow, orange and red vegetables have far more nutrients than pale ones. Hence, if you dislike pale zucchini, summer squash, and cucumbers, don't work hard to acquire a taste for them. Instead, put your efforts into having more broccoli, spinach and winter squash—the richly colored, more nutrient-dense choices.

- Include lettuce, tomato and onion on your sandwiches and wraps.

- Keep baby carrots and cherry tomatoes handy in the front of the refrigerator for easy snacking.

- Eat colorful salads filled with tomatoes, green peppers, carrots, spinach and dark lettuces. Pale salads with white lettuce, cucumbers, onions, celery and other pale veggies offer little more than crunch. When smothered with dressing, this crunch becomes highly caloric. Alternatives to a pale restaurant salad include tomato juice, vegetable soup, a steamed veggie or, when you get home, a handful of raw baby carrots for a bedtime snack.

- Fortify spaghetti sauce with a box of frozen chopped broccoli or green peppers. Cook the veggies alongside the spaghetti (in a steamer over the pasta water) before you add it to the tomato sauce.

- Choose fast foods with the most veggies:

  — Pizza with peppers, mushrooms and extra tomato sauce
  — Chinese entrées stir-fried with vegetables
  — Lunchtime V-8 juice instead of diet soda

- Even over-cooked vegetables are better than no vegetables. If your only option is over-cooked veggies from the cafeteria, eat them. While cooking does destroy some of the vegetable's nutrients, it does not destroy all of them. Any vegetable is better than no vegetable!

- Keep frozen vegetables stocked in your freezer, ready and waiting. They are quick and easy to prepare, won't spoil quickly, and have more nutrients than "fresh" vegetables that have been in the store and your refrigerator for a few days. Because cooking (more than freezing) reduces a vegetable's nutritional content:

  —quickly cook vegetables only until tender crisp and use the cooking water as a broth.
  — microwave vegetables in a covered dish.
  — stir-fry them with very little olive oil.

- Use a food processor to finely chop veggies to "hide" in meatloaf, soup and stews.

- When all else fails, eat fruit to help compensate for lack of vegetables. The best alternatives include bananas, oranges, grapefruit, melon, strawberries and kiwi. These choices are rich in many of the same nutrients found in vegetables.

For more information on serving sizes and ways to add more vegetables to your daily diet, see: www.MyPyramid.gov

Protein for Your Sports Diet

Like carbohydrates, protein-rich foods are also an important part of your sports diet. You should eat a protein-rich food at each meal. Runners tend to either *over-* or *under*consume protein, depending on their health consciousness and lifestyle. Whereas high-protein eaters frequently choose cheese omelets, fast food burgers and other meals filled with saturated fats, other runners bypass these foods in their efforts to eat a low-fat or vegetarian diet – but they often neglect to replace beef with beans. For additional information and guidelines on how to choose the best balance of protein, see Chapter 6: *Protein for Muscles.*

Recommended daily protein intake:
5 to 7 ounces (or ounce-equivalents; 140 to 200 g)

Protein-rich Foods	Runner's Portion	Number of ounces or ounce-equivalents
Tuna	6 oz. (170 g) can, drained	3-4
Chicken	6-ounce breast	6
Peanut Butter	2-4 tablespoons	1-2
Kidney Beans	1 cup	2

To meet your protein requirement for the day, you should consume not only one or two protein-rich foods per day but also the recommended two to three servings of calcium-rich dairy foods such as milk, yogurt and cheese (or other calcium-rich foods, such as calcium-fortified soy milk). Calcium is particularly important for growing teens and women who want to optimize bone density. For only 300 calories, even weight-conscious runners can easily achieve the recommended calcium intake – plus boost their protein intake – by consuming:
• 8 oz. (240 ml) of milk or soy milk on breakfast cereal
• 8 oz. (240 ml) tub of yogurt with lunch
• a (decaf) latte made with low-fat milk for an afternoon energizer

When choosing the recommended two to three daily servings of dairy foods, note that fat-free and low-fat products are preferable for heart-health and calorie control, but you need not suffer with skim milk if you really don't like it. You can always cut back on fat in other parts of your diet. For example, Margie, a first-year runner, opted for cereal with reduced-fat (2%) milk (five grams of fat per cup), but saved on fat elsewhere in her diet by using fat-free salad dressing and low-fat granola. (For more information on dietary fat, see Chapter 8.)

Runners who prefer a dairy-free diet or are lactose intolerant should take special care to eat adequate amounts of nondairy calcium sources. (See the chart below for food suggestions).

Calcium Equivalents

The recommended daily calcium intake is:

Age Group	Calcium (mg)
Teens, 9-18 years	1,300
Adults, 19-50 years	1,000
Adults, 51+ years	1,200-1,500

The following foods all provide about 300 milligrams of calcium. Three choices per day, or one at each meal, will contribute to meeting your calcium needs.

	Calcium-rich Foods	Amount	
Dairy	milk, whole or skim	1 cup	(240 ml)
	yogurt	1 cup	(230 g)
	cheese	1 1/2 ounces	(45 g)
	cottage cheese	2 cups	(450 g)
	frozen yogurt	1 1/2 cups	(150 g)
Proteins	soy milk	1 cup	(240 ml)
	tofu	8 oz.	(1/2 cake; 250 g)
	salmon, canned with bones	5 ounces	(140 g)
	sardines, canned with bones	3 ounces	(85 g)
	almonds	4 ounces	(110 g)
Vegetables	Broccoli, cooked	3 cups	(550 g)
	Collard or turnip greens, cooked	1 cup	(150 g)
	Kale or mustard greens, cooked	1 1/2 cups	(220 g)

Sweets and Treats

Although nutritionists recommend eating a wholesome diet based on grains, fruits and vegetables, some runners eat a diet with too many sweets and treats. If you have a junk-food diet, you may be able correct this imbalance by eating more wholesome foods *before you get too hungry*. Runners who get too hungry tend to choose sugary, fatty foods (such as apple pie, instead of apples). A simple solution to the junk-food diet is to *prevent* hunger by eating heartier portions of wholesome foods at meals.

Take note: you need not eat a "perfect diet" (*no* fats, *no* sugar) to have a good diet. Nothing is nutritionally wrong with having something sweet, such as a cookie for dessert after having eaten a sandwich, milk and fruit for lunch. But a lot is wrong with eating cookies for lunch and skipping the sandwich. That's when nutrition and performance problems arise.

The key to balancing fats and sugars appropriately in your diet is to abide by the following guidelines:
- *10 percent of your calories can appropriately come from refined sugar* (about 200-300 calories from sugar per day for most runners)
- *25 percent of your calories can appropriately come from (preferably healthful) fat* (about 450-750 calories from fat per day, or roughly 50-85 grams of fat per day)

Hence, moderate amounts of chips, cookies and ice cream can fit into an overall healthful food plan, if desired.

Need Some Help Shaping Up Your Diet?

If you want personalized dietary advice, I recommend you seek professional advice from a registered dietitian (RD) who specializes in sports nutrition and, ideally, is board-certified as a Specialist in Sports Dietetics (CSSD). To find a sports nutritionist in your area, use the referral networks on the American Dietetic Association's website (www.eatright.org) or the website of ADA's practice group of sports dietitians (www.SCANdpg.org). Or try googling "sports nutritionist, your city." You'll be glad you did! This personal nutrition coach can help you easily win with good nutrition.

Banana Bread

This recipe for banana bread is a favorite among runners of all ages and abilities. Spread peanut butter on a thick slice, add a glass of low fat milk and voilà—you've assembled a balanced meal that includes four food groups!

The trick to making good banana bread is to use well-ripened bananas. When you are confronted with bananas that are getting too ripe, use this recipe to solve the problem!

3	large bananas, the riper the better		
1	egg or 2 egg whites		
2	tbsp.	(30 ml)	oil, preferably canola
$1/3$ to $1/2$ cup		(70-100 g)	sugar
$1/4$	cup	(60 ml)	milk
1	tsp.	(5 g)	salt, as desired
1	tsp.	(5 g)	baking soda
$1/2$	tsp.	(2.5 g)	baking powder
$1 1/2$	cups	(180 g)	flour, preferably half white, half whole-wheat

1. Preheat oven to 350°F (175°C).
2. Spray a 9 x 5-inch (23 x 13 x 7-cm) loaf pan with cooking spray.
3. In a large bowl, mash the bananas with a fork.
4. Add the egg, oil, sugar, milk and salt. Beat well, and then add the baking soda and baking powder.
5. Gently blend the flour into the banana mixture. Stir for 20 seconds or until just moistened.
6. Pour the batter into the prepared pan.
7. Bake at 350°F (175°C) for 45 minutes or until a toothpick inserted near the middle comes out clean.

YIELD:	1 loaf, 12 slices
Nutritional Information	
Total calories:	1,600
Calories per slice:	140
Carbohydrates	24 g
Protein	3 g
Fat	3 g

Winning Recipe

Chapter 2
Breakfast: The Meal of Champions

If you want to "get it right" in terms of establishing a good sports diet, there's no doubt breakfast is *the* most important meal of the day! Yes, there are hurdles to eating breakfast, but the benefits far outweigh the costs. Breakfast eaters tend to:

- eat a more nutritious, lower fat diet.
- have lower blood cholesterol levels.
- enjoy success with weight control.
- be mentally alert and more productive.
- have more energy to enjoy exercise either in the morning or later that day.

As an up-and-coming runner, plan to start your day with breakfast within three hours of waking. From female runners on a 1,800-calorie weight reduction diet, to tall men who devour 3,600 calories a day, morning runners deserve to eat a hefty 500 to 900 calories for their morning meal(s). Morning runners do well by eating part of their breakfast before they run, and then enjoying the rest of the breakfast afterwards, either at home, on the way to work or at the office. (See Chapter 13 for information on how to calculate your calorie needs for breakfast and the entire day.)

Despite my clear message about breakfast being the most important meal of the day, I have to coax my clients to experiment with eating (more) breakfast. Far too many runners under-eat in the morning. Let's take at look at some standard breakfast excuses – and solutions.

I don't have time: Lack of *priority* is the real problem, not lack of time. If you can make time to run, you can make time to fuel for your run. Even if you choose to sleep to the last minute before dragging yourself out of bed to go to work, you can still choose to eat breakfast on the way to work or at the office. Some simple breakfasts to eat on the run include:
- a baggie filled with raisins, almonds and granola.
- a tortilla rolled with a slice or two of low-fat cheese.
- a peanut butter and honey sandwich on wholesome bread.
- a glass of milk, then a banana while walking to the bus or train.
- a travel mug filled with a fruit smoothie or protein shake (there will always be coffee at the office).
- an energy bar and a banana during the morning commute.

The key to breakfast on the run is to plan *ahead*. Prepare your breakfast the night before so that you can simply grab it and go during the morning rush. For example, on the weekends, you might want to make banana bread (see my favorite recipe at the end of Chapter 1) or buy a dozen bagels. Pre-slice the bread or the bagels, wrap the desired portion in individual plastic bags and put them in the freezer. Take one out of the freezer at night so breakfast will be ready and waiting in the morning.

Breakfast interferes with my training schedule: If you are an early morning runner (5:00–7:00 A.M.), you will likely exercise better and avoid an energy crash if you eat part of your breakfast before you exercise. (You might have to slowly train your stomach to tolerate this fuel.) Coffee with extra milk, a swig of juice, a chunk of bagel or piece of bread are popular choices that can get your blood sugar on the upswing, contribute to greater stamina and help you feel more awake. If you simply cannot tolerate this food, a bedtime snack the night before can reduce the risk of a morning energy lag. (Chapter 10: *Fueling Before You Run* explains in greater detail the importance of morning food.)

Breakfast is equally important if you run at mid-day or in the afternoon. You need to fuel up in order to do a quality workout later in the day.

"My favorite meal for breakfast before a long run is two pieces of whole grain toast with all natural jelly. I have never had any intestinal issues with this routine. Oatmeal is another successful choice."

Dave Poppel, Burlington, CT

I'm not hungry in the morning: If you have no morning appetite, the chances are you ate your breakfast calories the night before. Huge dinner? Ice cream? Too many cookies before bedtime? The solution to having no morning appetite is, obviously, to eat less at night so that you can start the day off hungry.

If running first thing in the morning "kills your appetite" (due to the rise in body temperature), keep in mind that you *will* be hungry within a few hours when you have cooled down. Plan ahead, so when the hungry horrors hit, you will have healthful options ready and waiting.

I'm on a diet: Too many weight-conscious people start their diets at breakfast. Bad idea. Breakfast skippers tend to gain weight and to be heavier than breakfast eaters. A satisfying breakfast *prevents you from getting too hungry* and over-eating later in the day.

Your best bet for successful dieting is to eat *during the day*, burn off the calories, and then eat a lighter meal at night. Chapter 14 has more details about how to lose weight and have energy to train.

"I still find it hard to believe that when I started eating more at breakfast and lunch, I lost weight. I felt as though I was cheating all the time. My running times even improved because I was actually well-fueled instead of half-starved."

Laura Perkins, New York City, NY

Breakfast makes me hungrier: Many runners complain that if they eat breakfast, they seem to get hungrier and eat more all day. This may result from thinking they have already "blown their diets" by eating breakfast, so they might as well keep overeating, then start dieting again the next day. Wrong. Successful diets start at breakfast.

If you feel hungry after breakfast you probably ate *too little* breakfast. For example, 100 calories of toast with jam is enough to whet your appetite but not to satisfy your calorie needs. Try budgeting about one-quarter of your calories for breakfast – 500–600 calories for most 120–150 pound runners. This translates into two slices of toast with jam, a banana, low-fat yogurt, *and* juice; or yogurt and a bagel with peanut butter.

Note: If you *overeat* at breakfast, you can easily resolve the problem by eating less at lunch or dinner. You won't be as physically hungry for those meals and will be able to easily eat smaller portions.

The Breakfast of Champions

By now, I hope I've convinced you that breakfast is indeed the most important meal of the day. *What* should you eat, you wonder?

I highly recommend cereal. Cereal is quick, convenient and filled with the calcium, iron, carbohydrates, fiber and other nutrients runners need. A bowl of whole grain cereal with fruit and low-fat milk provides a well-balanced meal that includes three of the four food groups (grain, milk and fruit) and sets the stage for an overall low-fat diet.

Nontraditional Breakfasts

Not everyone likes cereal for breakfast, nor do they want to cook eggs or pancakes. If what to eat for breakfast stumps you, choose a food that you enjoy. After all, you'll be more likely to eat breakfast if it tastes good. Remember that any food—even a cookie (preferably oatmeal raisin, rather than chocolate chip)—is better than nothing.

How about:
- leftover pizza
- leftover Chinese food
- mug of tomato soup
- potato zapped in the microwave while you take your shower
- tuna sandwich
- peanut butter and apple
- protein bar

Cereal is versatile. Mix brands and vary the flavor with different toppings:
- sliced banana
- blueberries (frozen ones taste great—especially if microwaved)
- raisins
- canned fruit
- cinnamon
- maple syrup
- vanilla yogurt

My personal favorite is to put a mix of cereals in a bowl, top it with fresh, frozen or canned fruit (depending on the season), heat it in the microwave oven for 30 to 60 seconds, and then add cold milk. It's like eating fruit cobbler!

How to Choose the Best Breakfast Cereal

Needless to say, all cereals are not created equal. By reading the Nutrition Facts on the cereal box, you can see that some offer more nutritional value than others. Also keep in mind hungry runners generally need more than one serving (a standard unit of measure) of cereal; they enjoy a larger portion (the amount chosen to satisfy the appetite) that contributes additional nutrients.

Here are four tips to help you make the best cereal choices.

1. **Choose iron-enriched cereals with at least 25 percent of the Daily Value for iron to help prevent anemia.**

   Note, however, the iron in breakfast cereals is poorly absorbed compared to the iron in lean red meats. But you can enhance iron absorption by drinking a glass of orange juice or enjoying another source of vitamin C (such as grapefruit, cantaloupe, strawberries or kiwi) along with the cereal. Any iron is better than no iron.

If you tend to eat "all-natural" types of cereals, such as granola and shredded wheat, be aware that these types have "no additives," hence no added iron. You might want to mix and match all-natural brands with iron-enriched brands (or make the effort to eat iron-rich foods at other meals).

2. **Choose fiber-rich bran cereals with more than 5 grams of fiber per serving.**
   Fiber not only helps prevent constipation, but also is a protective nutrient that may reduce your risk of colon cancer and heart disease. Whole grain and bran cereals offer the most fiber, more so than even fruits and vegetables. Choose from All-Bran, Raisin Bran, Bran Chex, Fiber One, or any of the numerous cereals with "bran" or "fiber" in the name. You can also mix high- and low-fiber cereals (Rice Crispies + Fiber One; Special K + Raisin Bran) to boost their fiber value.

Note: If you have trouble with diarrhea when running, you may want to forgo bran cereals. The extra fiber may aggravate the situation.

3. **Choose cereals with whole grains listed among the first ingredients.**
   Whole grains include whole wheat, brown rice, corn and oats; these should be listed first in the ingredients. In my opinion, you should pay more attention to a cereal's grain content than its sugar or sodium (salt) content. Sugar is a simple carbohydrate that fuels your muscles. Yes, sugar calories are nutritionally empty calories. But when they are combined with milk, banana and the cereal itself, the twenty empty calories in five grams of added sugar are insignificant. Obviously, sugar-filled frosted flakes and kids' cereals with fifteen grams of sugar or more per serving are somewhat more like dessert than breakfast. Hence, try to limit your breakfast choices to cereals with fewer than five grams of added sugar per serving. Enjoy the sugary ones for snacks or dessert, if desired, or mix a little with low-sugar cereals.

4. **Choose primarily low-fat cereals with less than two grams of fat per serving.**
   High-fat cereals such as some brands of granola and crunchy cookie-type cereals can add unexpected fat and calories to your sports diet. Select low-fat brands for the foundation of your breakfast, then use only a sprinkling of the higher-fat treats, if desired, for a topping.

Mix 'n Match Cereals

When it comes to cereals, you may not find one that meets all of your standards for high fiber, high iron and low fat, but you can always mix-and-match to create a winning combination.

Brand		Iron (%DV)	Fiber (g)	Fat (g)
The "Ideal cereal"		>25%	>5	<2
Cheerios, 1 cup	(30g)	45%	3	2
Wheaties, 1 cup	(30 g)	45%	3	1
Kashi Go Lean, 1 cup	(50 g)	10%	10	1
Raisin Bran, Kellogg's 1 cup	(60 g)	25%	7	1.5
Fiber One, 1/2 cup	(30 g)	25%	14	1
Quaker 100% Natural, 1/2 cup	(50 g)	6%	3	6
Oat Squares, Quaker, 1 cup	(60 g)	80%	4	2.5
Cap'n Crunch, 3/4 cup	(30 g)	25%	1	1.5

Going Out for Breakfast

At a restaurant, you can be confronted with fat-laden cheese omelets, hash browns and buttery toast. Take the higher carb route by ordering a fruit cup, oatmeal and whole-wheat toast. If you've done a long run, refuel with pancakes or French toast (request that butter be served on the side). Order a *large* orange juice or tomato juice, to help compensate for a potential lack of fruits or veggies in the other meals.

Summary

What you eat in the morning provides fuel for a high-energy day and stronger workouts. Breakfast helps novice and experienced runners alike to make their way to the winners' circle! Even dieting runners can enjoy breakfast without the fear of "getting fat" – that is, breakfast helps curb evening appetite so that dieters can eat lighter at night.

If you generally skip breakfast, at least give breakfast a try for two weeks. You'll soon learn why breakfast is the meal of champions!

Cold Cereal with Hot Fruit

Quick, easy and yummy! I love this combination of hot fruit with cereal and cold milk—it reminds me of fruit crisp à la mode. Bananas, pears, apples, berries… any and all fruits work well. The same goes for the choice of cereals. Be creative!

This recipe also works well with fresh, frozen or canned fruits. For example, I generally stock blueberries in the freezer, so they are ready and waiting to be enjoyed for breakfast. Then any day I can make "blueberry crisp" for breakfast by simply shaking a handful onto the cold cereal and heating them up.

In the winter, having warm fruit takes the cold chill away from the quick-and-easy cereal breakfast. It's easier than cooking hot cereal, and offers the same warm glow after a chilly morning run.

1 cup	(100 g)	Life cereal or Oat Squares
$^1/_2$ cup	(50 g)	All-Bran or Fiber-One
$^1/_4$ cup	(22 g)	low-fat granola
$^1/_2$ cup	(75 g)	blueberries or other fruit
1 cup	(240 ml)	low-fat milk

1. In a microwaveable bowl, combine the cereals.

2. Sprinkle with blueberries or other fruit of your choice.

3. Heat in the microwave oven for 20 to 40 seconds, until the blueberries are warm.

4. Pour the cold milk over the top. Dig in!

Yield:	1 serving
Nutrition Information:	
Total calories:	500
Carbohydrate:	85
Protein:	20
Fat:	7

Reprinted with permission from Nancy Clark's Sports Nutrition Guidebook, Fourth Edition (Human Kinetics, 2008)

Chapter 3
Lunch, Snacks and Dinner

Whereas breakfast is the most important meal of your training diet, lunch is the second most important. In fact, I encourage runners to eat TWO lunches – one lunch at 11:00 am, when you first start to get hungry, then a second lunch at 3:00 to 4:00 pm, when the munchies strike. If you train in the morning, these lunches refuel your muscles. If you train in the late afternoon, these lunches prepare you for a strong workout. And in either case, two lunches curb your appetite so you are not starving at the end of the day and have the energy to cook a nutritious dinner.

I invite you to experiment with this two-lunch concept. If you are like most of my clients, you'll find yourself looking forward to a second sandwich to boost your energy at the end of the day. Afraid that two lunches will be fattening? Fear not; a second lunch does not mean additional calories. You'll simply be trading your afternoon cookies and evening ice cream for a wholesome afternoon meal. No longer will you search for evening snacks; you ate them earlier.

What's for Lunch?

Runners commonly have three options for lunch: pack your own, pick up some fast food or enjoy a hot meal from the cafeteria at work or school. You can eat healthfully in each of these scenarios; just remember to enjoy three kinds of wholesome food with each meal (bread + peanut butter + banana; pizza crust + tomato sauce + cheese; chicken + rice + vegetables) and at least 500 to 600 calories per meal (based on a 2,000 to 2,400 calorie food plan, the amount appropriate for runners who want to lose weight; non-dieters can target about 600 to 800 calories per meal).

Eating a hot meal in the middle of the day can make the evening easier for runners who train in the late afternoon, arrive home starved and don't feel like cooking. Enjoying a nice meal at noon can also make a simple soup-and-sandwich dinner more acceptable. For hot meal suggestions, see the section on Dinner and Runners on page 37.

Pack-your-own Lunches

Packing your own lunch is a good way to save money, time and oftentimes saturated fat and calories if you are organized enough to have the right foods on hand. Good nutrition certainly starts in the supermarket! One trick to packing your lunch is to schedule "food shopping" into your training log. A second trick is to make lunch the night before.

The following suggestions may help you pack a super sports lunch.
- To prevent sandwich bread from getting stale, keep it in the freezer and take out the slices as needed. Bread thaws in minutes at room temperature, or in seconds in the microwave oven.

- Make several sandwiches at one time, then store them in the freezer. The frozen sandwich will be thawed – and fresh – by lunchtime. Sliced turkey, lean roast beef, peanut butter and leftover pizza freeze nicely. Don't freeze eggs, mayonnaise, jelly, lettuce, tomatoes or raw veggies.

- Instead of eating a dry sandwich with no mayonnaise, add moistness using low-fat mayonnaise, low-fat bottled salad dressings such as ranch or creamy Italian, mustard or ketchup, lettuce and tomato.

- Return to eating peanut butter; it is filled with health-protective fat that reduces your risk of heart disease and diabetes. Enjoy peanut butter (or other nut butters) with sliced banana, raisins, dates, sunflower seeds, apple slices and/or celery slices.

- Add zip to a (low-fat) cheese sandwich with oregano, Italian seasonings, green peppers and/or tomatoes.

- Pack leftover soups, chili and pasta dinners for the next day's lunch. You can either eat the leftovers cold, or heat them in the office microwave oven.

"Create a shopping list of nutritious, tasty and ready-to-eat foods. Keep your refrigerator, pantry, purse, office and/or car stocked with these foods so that you don't go hungry and end up raiding the vending machine."

Vivian Adkins, Potomac, MD

Going Out for Lunch

Quick-service and family restaurants now offer more low-fat foods than ever before. But, you'll still be confronted by the fatty temptations (burgers, fried fish, special sandwiches and French fries) that jump out at you. Before succumbing to grease, remind yourself that you will feel better and feel better about yourself if you eat well.

Here are suggestions for some lower-fat choices:

Dunkin' Donuts: Low-fat muffin, bagel, juice, bean or broth-based soups, hot cocoa.

Deli: Bagel with bean- or broth-based soups, sandwiches or subs with lots of bread and half the roast beef, turkey, ham or cheese. (Or, ask for two extra slices of bread or a second roll to make a sandwich for your second lunch with the excessive meat.) Hold the mayonnaise; instead add moistness with mustard or ketchup, sliced tomatoes and lettuce. Add more carbohydrates with juice, fruit, fig bars or yogurt for dessert.

McDonald's: Grilled chicken sandwich, yogurt parfait, salad with dressing on the side.

Wendy's: Bowl of chili with a plain baked potato.

Taco Bell: Bean burrito.

Pizza: Thick-crust with extra veggies rather than extra cheese or pepperoni.

Pasta: Spaghetti or ziti with tomato sauce and a glass of low-fat milk for protein. Be cautious of lasagna, tortellini or manicotti that are filled with cheese (i.e., high in saturated fat).

Chinese: Hot and sour or wonton soup, plain rice with stir-fried entrées such as beef and broccoli or chicken with pea pods. Request the food be cooked with minimal oil. Limit fried appetizers and fried entrées.

Soups: Hearty soups (such as split pea, minestrone, lentil, vegetable or noodle) accompanied by crackers, bread, a plain bagel or an English muffin provide a satisfying, carbohydrate-rich, low-fat meal.

Beverages: Both juices and soft drinks are rich in carbohydrates that fuel muscles. Juices, however, are better for your health, offering vitamin C, potassium and wholesome goodness.

Salad for Lunch

Salads, whether served as a main dish or an accompaniment, are a simple way to boost your intake of fresh vegetables—That's good! But as a runner, you need a substantial, carbohydrate-based lunch; most salads get the bulk of their calories from salad oil—Bad! You'll be better able to fuel your muscles if you choose a sandwich with a side salad for lunch, rather than only eating a big salad for the entire meal.

Three tricks to making a healthy sports salad are:
1. Choose a variety of colorful vegetables – dark green lettuces, red tomatoes, yellow peppers, orange carrots – for a variety of vitamins and minerals. If the vegetables you buy for salads tend to wilt in your refrigerator, consider frequent trips to the salad bar at the grocery store and deli as an alternative to tossing veggies that spoil before you find the chance to eat them.

2. Add extra carbohydrates:
   • dense vegetables, such as corn, peas, beets, carrots
   • beans and legumes, such as chickpeas, kidney beans, and three-bean salad
   • cooked rice or pasta
   • oranges, apples, raisins, grapes, craisins
   • toasted croutons
   • whole-grain bread or roll on the side

3. Monitor the dressing. Some runners drown 50 calories of healthful salad ingredients with 400 calories of blue cheese dressing! At a restaurant, always request the dressing be served on the side. Otherwise, you may get 400 calories of oil or mayonnaise—fatty foods that fill your stomach but leave your muscles unfueled.
   If you choose to use regular dressings, try to select ones made with olive oil for both a nice flavor and health-protective monounsaturated fats. If you want to reduce your fat intake, simply dilute regular dressings with water, more vinegar, or even milk (in ranch and other mayonnaise-based dressings). Or, choose from the plethora of low-fat and fat-free salad dressings. Low-fat dressings are good not only for salads, but also sandwiches, baked potatoes and dips.

Salads

Here is a comparison of some popular salad ingredients. Note that the ones with the most color have the most nutritional value.

Salad Ingredient Daily Value	Vitamin C (mg) 60 mg	Vitamin A (IU) 5,000 IU	Magnesium (mg) 400 mg
Broccoli, 5" (13 cm) stalk (180 g)	110	2,500	24
Green pepper, 1/2 (70 g)	65	210	20
Spinach, 2 cups raw (110 g)	50	8,100	90
Tomato, medium (12 g)	25	760	15
Romaine, 2 cups (110 g)	30	3,000	10
Iceberg, 2 cups (110 g)	5	360	5
Cucumber, 1/2 medium (150 g)	10	325	15
Celery, 1 stalk (40 g)	5	55	4

Solving the Four O'Clock Munchies Problem

Many runners believe eating in the afternoon is sinful. They self-inflict "Thou shalt not snack" as an Eleventh Commandment. Then, they succumb and feel guilty. As I have mentioned before, hunger is simply your body's request for fuel. Hunger is neither bad nor wrong. It is a normal physiological function. You can expect to get hungry every 4 hours. For example, if you eat lunch at noon, you can appropriately be hungry by 4:00. Eat something—preferably a second lunch!

"Second lunch" conjures up visions of real food—a second sandwich, a mug of soup, or peanut butter on crackers and a (decaf) latte. In comparison, "afternoon snack" suggests candy, cookies and sweets. Runners who fail to eat enough at breakfast and first lunch generally crave afternoon sweets. The preferred solution to sweet cravings is not to eat chocolate, but to prevent the cravings by eating more food earlier in the day and a second lunch later in the afternoon.

A second lunch is particularly important for dieters. As I will discuss in Chapter 14, a *planned* afternoon lunch of 300 to 500 calories (or whatever fits into your calorie budget) will prevent extreme hunger and reduce the risk of blowing your diet.

Second Lunch Suggestions

Some runners enjoy a second sandwich for their second lunch. But others like to graze on two or three wholesome snacks from this list. Whatever you do, plan ahead and have healthful options ready and waiting. That way, you can avoid the temptations that lurk in every convenience store, vending machine or bakery.

For your second lunch, try to pick items from two or three different food groups, such as carrots + cottage cheese + crackers; or graham crackers + peanut butter + apple.

Perishable snacks to carry with you or buy fresh:	Nonperishable snacks to keep stocked in your desk drawer:
• whole wheat bagel	• cold cereal (by the handful right out of the box or in a bowl with milk)
• low-fat bran muffin	
• microwaved potato	• hot cereal (packets of instant oatmeal are easy)
• yogurt, low-fat	
• cottage cheese, low-fat	• reduced-fat microwave popcorn
• cheese sticks, low-fat	• canned soup (preferably reduced sodium)
• thick-crust pizza	• canned tuna
• fresh fruit	• low-fat crackers (Ak-Mak, Wasa, Melba Toast)
• baby carrots	• graham crackers
• leftover pasta	• low-fat granola bars
• frozen meal	• energy bars
• peanut butter sandwich	• juice boxes or bottles
	• dried fruit
	• peanut butter
	• nuts, trail mix

Vending machine snacks: Vending-machine cuisine offers tough choices. But tucked between the lackluster choices, you may be able to find pretzels, peanuts, juice, yogurt or even an apple. The good part about vending-machine snacks is that they are limited in size (e.g., only three cookies instead of the whole bag) and generally provide only 200 to 400 calories, not 2,000.

If trying to decide between fatty or sugary choices (i.e., chips vs. jelly beans), remember that the sugar in jelly beans will appropriately fuel your muscles (but not satisfy your hunger), whereas the fat in the chips will clog the arteries. (After eating a sugary snack, be sure to brush or rinse your teeth.)

Cookie Monster snacks: If it's cookies, brownies, an ice cream sundae, or any other such treat that you crave once a week or so, I recommend you satisfy your hankering by enjoying the treat in place of one of your lunches. Simply trade in your lunch-calories for treat-calories, so you won't be overeating. You won't destroy your health with an occasional treat, as long as your overall diet tends to be wholesome. Looking at the weekly picture, you want to target a diet that averages 90% quality foods, 10% treats, if desired.

Healthful snacks and munchies: To reduce the temptation of the vending machine, keep handy a supply of wholesome options: whole-grain bagels, crackers, pretzels, fig bars, energy bars, granola bars, oatmeal-raisin cookies, graham crackers, raisins and other dried fruit, trail mix, V-8 juice and juice boxes.

Dinner and Runners

Dinnertime generally marks the end of the workday, a time to relax and enjoy a pleasant meal, that is, if you have the energy to prepare it. The trick to dining on a balanced dinner—the protein-starch-vegetable kind that mom used to make with at least three kinds of foods—is to arrive home with enough *energy* to cook. This means fueling your body and brain with adequate calories prior to dinnertime—with a second lunch.

If you are far from being a master chef, you might want to take a cooking class at your local center for adult education. But no number of cooking classes will help if you arrive home too hungry to cook or make wise food choices.

"I keep boxes of frozen chopped broccoli and spinach in my freezer. They quickly thaw in the microwave oven and add nutrients and flavor to pizza and pasta entrees."

Natalie Updegrove Partridge, Washington DC

Quick Fixes: Dinner Tips for Hungry Runners

Because good nutrition starts in the supermarket, you have a far better chance of achieving a super sports diet when your kitchen is well stocked with appropriate foods. You might want to muster up your energy to marathon shop at the discount or warehouse food store once every two or three weeks and *really shop*, so that you have enough food to last for a while. To help accomplish this goal, post a copy of the *Runner's Basic Shopping List* (see below) on your refrigerator and check off the foods you need.

Runner's Basic Shopping List

Keep this on your refrigerator and be sure to notice when an item gets low and needs to be replaced.

Cupboard: cereal, spaghetti, spaghetti sauce, brown rice, whole grain crackers, baked corn chips, kidney beans, baked beans, refried beans, tuna (canned or in a foil pouch), salmon (canned or in a foil pouch), peanut butter, soups (such as mushroom for making casseroles; lentil, minestrone, hearty bean), baking potatoes, V-8 or other vegetable juices.

Refrigerator: low-fat Cheddar, mozzarella and cottage cheese, low-fat milk and (Greek) yogurt, Parmesan cheese, eggs, tofu, tortillas, carrots, lettuce, tomatoes, oranges, bananas (when refrigerated, the banana peel turns black but the fruit itself is fine and lasts longer).

Freezer: whole-grain bagels, whole-wheat pita, English muffins, multigrain bread, orange juice concentrate, broccoli, spinach, winter squash, ground turkey, extra-lean hamburger, chicken (pieces frozen individually in baggies).

By keeping your kitchen well stocked with basic foods, you will have the makings for simple meals such as:

- Spaghetti with tomato sauce plus hamburger, ground turkey, tofu, beans, cheese cottage, grated cheese and/or vegetables

- English muffin or pita pizzas

- Tuna noodle casserole

- Soup and sandwiches (tuna, toasted cheese, peanut butter with banana)

- Microwaved potato topped with cottage cheese, baked beans or yogurt

- Peanut butter crackers and V-8 juice

- Bean burritos (frozen, or made with canned refried beans, salsa and tortilla)

Some runners use their morning shower/shave time to cook 1 $\frac{1}{2}$ cups of raw rice while getting ready for work. Come dinnertime, they simply brown one pound of lean hamburger or ground turkey in a large skillet, dump in the cooked rice and then add whatever vegetable is handy. Cooking 1 $\frac{1}{2}$ cups of raw rice for each pound of raw lean meat generates two generous sports meals with 60 percent of the calories from carbohydrates.

Some popular creations with rice and ground meat include:

- Mexican—canned beans + chili powder + grated low-fat cheddar cheese + diced tomatoes

Quick and Easy Meal Ideas
Here are some ideas for quick-and-easy meals:
- pasta with clam sauce, tomato sauce, frozen vegetables and/or low fat cheese
- canned beans, rinsed and then spooned over rice, pasta, or salads
- frozen dinners, supplemented with whole-grain bread and fresh fruit
- Pierogies, tortellini and burritos from the frozen food section
- baked potato topped with cottage cheese
- whole-grain cereal (hot or cold) with fruit and low-fat milk
- thick-crust pizza, fresh or frozen, then reheated in the toaster oven
- bean soups, homemade, canned or from the deli
- quick-cooking brown rice—made double for the next day's rice and bean salad
- stir-fry, using precut vegetables from the market, salad bar or freezer

- Chinese—broccoli zapped in the microwave oven while the meat cooks + soy sauce
- Italian—green beans + Italian seasonings such as basil, oregano and garlic powder
- American—grated low-fat cheddar cheese + onion browned with the meat + diced tomatoes

Pasta and Runners

Every runner regardless of language understands the word pasta. Pasta is popular not only before a marathon, but also as a standard part of the training diet. Even runners who claim they can't cook can manage to boil pasta in one shape or another. Some choose to eat pasta at least five nights of the week thinking it is a kind of superfood—Wrong.

Granted, pasta is carbohydrate-rich, quick and easy to cook, heart-healthy, economical, fun to eat and enjoyed by just about every member of the family. But in terms of vitamins, minerals and protein, plain pasta is a lackluster food. Here's some information to help you to place pasta in perspective.

Nutritional Value: Pasta is an excellent source of carbohydrates for muscle fuel and is the equivalent of "gas" for your engine. But plain pasta is a marginal source of vitamins and minerals, the "spark plugs" you need for top performance. Pasta is simply made from refined white flour—the same stuff you get in "wonder breads"—with a few vitamins added to replace those lost during processing. Even whole-wheat pastas offer little nutritional superiority, because wheat (and other grains in general) is better respected for its carbohydrate-value than its vitamins and minerals. Spinach and tomato pastas also get overrated since they contain relatively little spinach or tomato in comparison to having a serving of that vegetable along with the meal.

Pasta's nutritional value comes primarily from the sauces:
- tomato sauce rich in vitamins A and C and potassium
- pesto-type sauces rich in vitamins A and C and potassium
- clam sauce rich in protein, zinc and iron.

Be cautious with pasta smothered with butter, cream or greasy meat sauces. Creamy, cheesy pastas can be artery-clogging nutritional nightmares.

Pasta and Protein: Pasta is popular not only for carbohydrates but also for being a vegetarian alternative to meat-based meals. However, many runners live on too much pasta and neglect their protein needs. To boost the protein-value of tomato sauce, add:

- 2–3 ounces of extra-lean ground beef or turkey
- $^1/_4$ cup of grated low-fat mozzarella cheese
- $^1/_2$ cake tofu
- $^1/_2$ cup canned, drained kidney beans
- 3 ounces tuna (one-half of a 6-ounce can)
- $^1/_2$ cup of canned minced clams
- 1 cup of low-fat cottage cheese

Or, instead of adding protein to the sauce, drink two glasses of low-fat milk with the meal.

Pasta with added protein is also a wise choice, particularly for vegetarians and non-meat eaters.

Summary

If you are like many runners who struggle with eating well on a daily basis, please remember the following keys to a successful sports diet:

1. Eat appropriately sized meals on a regular schedule so that you won't get too hungry. Notice how your lunches and dinner deteriorate when you eat too little breakfast and get too hungry.

2. Spend your calories on a variety of wholesome foods at each meal; target at least three kinds of food per meal.

3. Pay attention to how much better you feel, run and feel about yourself when you eat a well-balanced sports diet.

It's my opinion that getting too hungry is the biggest problem with most runners' diets. A hearty breakfast sets the stage for a top-notch sports diet, and a second lunch paves the way to a healthful dinner.

Winning Recipe

Easy Enchilada Casserole

Here's a family favorite recipe with ingredients you can easily keep stocked in the cupboard and freezer. It's easy to prepare, and satisfying for hungry runners.

This particular recipe includes ground beef, but you could just as easily make it with ground turkey, diced tofu or kidney beans. For color, top the casserole with diced peppers.

1 pound	(450 g)	extra lean ground beef
28-ounce	(800 g)	can diced tomatoes, drained (or fresh tomatoes, chopped)
10-ounce	(250 g)	can enchilada sauce
16-ounce	(450 g)	can refried beans, preferably low fat
6 ounces	(150 g)	baked corn chips
4 ounces	(115 g)	cheddar cheese, preferably reduced fat

Optional: 1 medium onion, chopped; 1 teaspoon chili powder; $^1/_2$ teaspoon dried basil; 1 green pepper, diced

1. Brown the ground beef (and onion) in a large nonstick skillet.

2. Drain any fat, and then add the diced tomatoes, enchilada sauce and refried beans (and chili and basil, as desired). Heat until bubbly.

3. Preheat the oven to 350°F (175°C). Crumble the corn chips and spread all but 1 cup in the bottom of a 9 x 13-inch (33 x 23 x 5-cm) baking pan.

4. Pour the enchilada-beef sauce over the chips.

5. Grate the cheese and sprinkle it over the enchilada-beef sauce. Sprinkle with 1 cup corn chips (and diced green pepper, if desired).

6. Bake for 15 minutes or until the cheese is melted.

Yield:	6 servings
Nutrition Information:	
Total calories:	2,800
Calories per serving:	470
Carbohydrate:	52 g
Protein:	30 g
Fat:	16 g

Reprinted with permission from Nancy Clark's Sports Nutrition Guidebook, Fourth Edition (Human Kinetics, 2008)

Chapter 4
Vitamins and Supplements for Runners

Vitamins are essential food components that your body can't make. They perform important jobs in your body, including helping to convert food into energy. (Vitamins do not provide energy, however.) As a hungry runner who requires more food than the average person, you can easily consume large doses of vitamins in, let's say, a taller glass of orange juice or bigger pile of steamed broccoli. Chapter 1 has information about some of the best food sources of vitamins.

Because food consumption surveys suggest that many people fail to eat a well-balanced variety of wholesome foods, some runners may indeed suffer from marginal nutritional deficiencies, particularly those who restrict calories or skimp on fruits, vegetables and dairy foods. Yet, despite the rising popularity of supplements, many health organizations, including the American Heart Association and the National Institutes of Health, recommend food, not pills, for optimal nutrition. That's because whole food contains far more than just vitamins. It contains carbs, protein, phytochemicals, fiber and other health-protective substances that are not in pills. Hence, the key to good health is to learn how to eat well regardless of your lifestyle.

"Vitamin pills are great, but there's no substitute for the real thing."

Jonathan Dietrich, Washington, DC

Runners who eat vitamin-enriched foods such as energy bars and breakfast cereals commonly consume far more vitamins than they realize. But take note: Runners who eat primarily "all natural foods" from the whole foods stores miss out on the benefit of enriched foods. ("All natural foods" have no added vitamins or minerals, like B-vitamins and iron.) That's one reason why the government food guidelines acknowledge that some of our grains can appropriately come from enriched foods.

To date, no studies have documented a physiological need for mega-doses of vitamins for runner, marathoners and other athletes. Yet, supplements are indeed appropriate for certain populations, including:
- folic acid for pregnant women and women who *might* become pregnant (expectedly or unexpectedly), to prevent certain birth defects.
- iron for vegetarians and women with heavy menstrual periods.
- zinc and anti-oxidants for nonsmokers with macular degeneration (an eye disease).
- vitamin D for people (like gym rats) who get very little sunlight.

If you choose to take a supplement for its potential health-protective effects, be sure to do so *in addition to eating well*. Researchers have yet to unravel the whole vitamin/health mystery, so stay tuned and be sure to take care of your whole health with the vitamins, phytochemicals, omega-3 fats and other unknown substances found in whole foods.

Vitamins for Fatigue?

Some runners complain of chronic fatigue. They feel run down, dragged out and overwhelmingly exhausted. They come to me wondering if something is wrong with their diet—and if taking vitamins would solve the problem. Here are some questions I ask to help decipher the source of their energy problems.

- *Are you tired due to low blood sugar?* If you skimp on breakfast, miss lunch because you "don't have time" and then doze off in the afternoon because you have low blood sugar, no amount of vitamins will solve that energy problem! You need to choose to make time to eat lunch, and choose to stock wholesome snacks (nuts, dried fruit) at the office.

- *Is your diet too low in carbohydrates?* If you eat too many fast-but-fatty food choices, you will fill your stomach but leave your muscles poorly fueled with inadequate glycogen to support your training program. You'll run with "dead legs."

- *Are you iron-deficient and anemic?* If you eat little red meat and consequently little iron, you might be low in this important mineral in red blood cells that helps carry oxygen to exercising muscles. Iron-deficiency anemia can result in needless fatigue during exercise. To boost your dietary iron intake, with or without meat, see chapter 7. You might also want to talk with your doctor about getting your blood tested (hemoglobin, hematocrit, ferritin, serum iron and total iron-binding capacity) to rule out the question of anemia.

- *Are you getting enough sleep?* Perhaps you are simply burning the candle at both ends and are rightfully tired. While advice to "get more sleep" is easier said than done, you can strive to make sleep more of a priority on your "to do" list.

- *Are you overtraining?* Some novice runners think their running will improve faster if they train as hard as possible very day. Wrong! One or two rest days or easy days per week are an essential part of a training program; they provide the time the body needs to replenish depleted muscle glycogen.

- *Are you stressed or depressed?* When life is feeling out of control, life's stresses can certainly drain your mental energy, create sleep problems and leave you feeling exhausted. Choosing to eat healthful meals on a regular schedule can help you feel better both physically and mentally. That is energizing in itself.

For most runners, resolving fatigue with better eating, sleeping, and training habits is more effective than taking vitamin pills. By implementing the simple food suggestions in this book, you can transform low-energy eating patterns into a fueling plan for success! Eating well is not as hard as you may think.

For more Information

Confusion abounds regarding dietary supplements, their safety, and their potential health benefits. Here are some websites that offer abundant information about vitamins and health. (You might need to do a search on "vitamins" or "fish oil" to find your topic of interest):

The American Heart Association:
www.americanheart.org

FDA's Center for Food Safety and Applied Nutrition:
www.cfsan.fda.gov

National Library of Medicine:
www.nlm.nih.gov/medlineplus

The World's Healthiest Foods:
www.whfoods.org

Summary

Your best bet for fighting fatigue is to be responsible with your food choices and nourish your body with the right balance of wholesome foods. Make the effort to eat a variety of foods and fluids from the different food groups every day to consume not only the amounts of the vitamins and minerals you need, but also the calories your body needs to prevent fatigue.

If you are tempted to take supplements for health insurance, do so only if you simultaneously choose to eat responsibly. Remember, no amount of supplements will compensate for an inadequate diet—but you will always win with good nutrition. Eat wisely, eat well!

A Super Salad with Sweet and Spicy Dressing

A colorful salad is a super way to eat a portfolio of nutrient-dense foods and boost your nutrient intake. Here's a suggestion for a super salad that is a meal in itself, rich in not only vitamins, but also protein (to build muscles), carbs (to fuel muscles), fiber (to move food through your system) and healthful fats to help fight inflammation.

In a large bowl, combine your choice of colorful salad vegetables, such as:

• Spinach	• Red pepper	• Carrot
• Tomato	• Yellow pepper	• Dark green Lettuce

Add protein and healthful fat:

• Flaked tuna or canned salmon	• Chopped walnuts or slivered almonds

Include some calcium-rich food:

• Shredded lowfat cheese	• Tofu cubes	• Lowfat cottage cheese

Accompany with your choice of wholesome carbs:

• Whole wheat English muffin	• Fresh rolls
• Toasted whole grain bread	• Whole grain crackers

Sweet and Spicy Dressing

Here's a dressing that will have you licking the salad bowl clean! It goes very well with salads with a spinach base.

3 tablespoons	45 g	olive oil
2 tablespoons	30 g	red wine vinegar
1 tablespoon	15 g	sugar
1 teaspoon	5 g	salt as desired
1 tablespoon	15 g	ketchup

1. In a jar combine the olive oil, vinegar, sugar, salt, and ketchup. Cover and shake until well blended.
2. Add a little dressing to the salad; toss well.

Yield:	dressing for 4 large salads
Nutritional Information:	
Total calories:	400
calories per serving:	100
carb:	4 g
Protein:	0 g
Fat:	9 g

Chapter 5
Food and Exercise: Better than Medicine

As a new runner, you are taking big steps to invest in your health. There's no question that—
- good nutrition combined with regular running is more powerful than medicine for improving and protecting your health.
- being fit overpowers being fat when it comes to protecting your health.

This means, if you have excess body fat but are fit, you will likely live longer than your peers who are fat but not fit. If you are fat and fit, you'll likely live longer than thin people who are unfit. Whatever you do, stay active throughout your lifetime!

Many of the diseases of aging—high blood pressure, heart disease, stroke, obesity, osteoporosis, diabetes, and some cancers—are related to inactivity and overnutrition; these diseases are common among people who are sedentary and overweight. By running and fueling your body with quality nutrition, you can counter these health risks. Running is certainly a smart investment in your current and future well-being!

In combination with running, be sure to enjoy wholesome foods; they are like powerful drugs and are more effective than many medicines. Both the American Heart Association and the American Cancer Society recommend we counter heart disease and cancer by eating larger portions of fruits, vegetables and whole grains, and smaller portions of fatty meats.

The following information highlights the power of exercise and good nutrition and will hopefully inspire you to eat wisely, run regularly, and invest in your future well-being.

"Treating the body like a brand new Cadillac instead of a used, rusting Ford will definitely give you more miles with fewer problems in the long run."

Paula Sue Russell, Findlay, OH

Obesity

If you are significantly overweight, starting an exercise program (initially strength training to get stronger, and then walking, jogging and eventually running) is the best thing you can do to invest in your health. There's little doubt that having excess body fat is associated with an increased risk of developing Type 2 diabetes, high blood pressure and heart disease. If you can lose even a small amount of weight—5 to 7% of your body weight, which is 10 to 14 pounds for a 200 pound person—you will gain incredible health benefits. (Yes, you can consider even that small amount of weight loss as being "successful"!)

How much do you need to run to improve your health? Not much. Both the American College of Sports Medicine and the American Heart Association recommend a minimum of 30 minutes of moderate-intensity physical activity five days a week or 20 minutes of vigorous-intensity physical activity three days a week, or a combination of the two. Because vigorous running comes with the possibility of getting injured, having less fun (i.e., poor adherence), and "burning out," your best bet is to enjoy running (or walking) at an enjoyable pace. That way, you will be more likely to sustain your running program and—

- lower your cholesterol and triglycerides.

- improve your blood glucose clearance.

- reduce your risk of having a heart attack.

- lose body fat *if* the exercise contributes to a calorie deficit for the day. (Please see Chapter 14 for weight reduction information.)

Diabetes

People who are overweight and underfit are at high risk for developing Type II diabetes, a condition associated with heart attacks, stroke, kidney disease, blindness and amputation of limbs. Yikes—start running! Running improves the effectiveness of insulin, the hormone that helps transport sugar (glucose) from the blood into the muscles. High levels of blood glucose contribute to the health complications mentioned above.

If you are lugging around excess body fat, you are at risk for being *insulin resistant*. That means you have a reduced ability for insulin to do its job of transporting sugar out of the blood and into the muscles. Insulin resistant cells respond less to the action of insulin. As a result, the pancreas secretes even larger amounts of insulin in an effort to get glucose into the cells, and that creates medical problems.

To find out if you are insulin resistant, talk with your doctor about having some blood tests to measure your blood glucose both after an overnight fast and after a specific dose of sugar. If you are insulin resistant, you'll want to lose weight (assuming you are overweight); exercise regularly for 30 to 45 minutes a day; and eat a healthful diet based on fruits, vegetables, whole grains and lean protein, especially fish. Include healthful monounsaturated fats such as olive and canola oil, nuts and avocado.

If the insulin resistance (pre-diabetes) has progressed to full-blown diabetes, you want to work with a registered dietitian for personalize advice. (Use the referral network at www.eatright.org.) You might also want to read the *Diabetic Athlete's Handbook* (Sheri Colberg, Human Kinetics 2008) for in-depth advice, and check the American Diabetes Association's website, www.diabetes.org.

The good news is, even small changes in physical activity and weight can improve insulin resistance and reduce its negative health consequences. So start running (or walking or lifting weights) and develop a program that is do-able and sustainable.

Cancer

Lack of fitness is second only to cigarette smoking as a preventable cause of cancer. People who are underfit and overfat are at high risk for developing cancer, in particular, cancer of the breast, endometrium, colon and pancreas. If you are overweight, underfit, and insulin resistant, your pancreas will secrete even larger amounts of insulin in an effort to get glucose into the cells. That raises levels of hormones known to feed the growth of cancer cells.

The 2007 report on "Food, Nutrition, Physical Activity and the Prevention of Cancer: A Global Perspective" recommends "being physically active for at least 30 minutes every day" as one way to prevent cancer. The following list highlights some dietary suggestions to reduce your cancer risk.

1. Be as lean as possible without becoming underweight. See Chapter 14 for detailed information on how to lose weight yet maintain energy to run.

2. To manage your weight, avoid sugary drinks—this includes limiting sports drinks to only during exercise that lasts longer than 60 to 90 minutes—and limit your intake of energy-dense foods (particularly processed foods high in added sugar, low in fiber or high in fat, such as ice cream, cookies, chips and most sweets and treats).

3. Eat more of a variety of vegetables, fruits, whole grains and beans/legumes. To integrate more beans into your meals:

   • Mix kidney beans with rice.

   • Replace potato with refried beans.

   • Add garbanzos to your salad instead of croutons.

   • Enjoy hummus instead of mayonnaise on your turkey sandwich.

   • To integrate more fruits and vegetables, review Chapters 1, 2 and 3.

4. Eat more whole grains. For example:

   • Make oatmeal a regular breakfast choice.

   • Replace white rice with brown rice.

   • Snack on whole grain cereal bars, like Kashi Bars or Clif Bars

   • Enjoy popcorn, preferably home-popped in a small amount of canola oil.

5. Eat smaller portions of red meats (such as juicy steaks and greasy burgers) and avoid processed meats (such as hot dogs, bologna and pepperoni).

6. If consumed at all, limit alcoholic drinks to 2 for men and 1 for women a day.

7. Limit your intake of salty foods and processed foods high in sodium (such as boxed macaroni & cheese, canned soups and salty chips). High salt intake can damage the lining of the stomach and increase the risk of developing stomach cancer.

8. Don't expect supplements to protect against cancer. Real foods offer an array of health protective compounds that are missing from supplements.

For more complete information on how to eat to reduce your risk of developing cancer, see www.aicr.org.

"My food mantra: Eat like a caveman. Foods in their simplest, most original form are best for your health!"

Jessica Hendren, Chicago, IL

Heart Disease

You are at risk of heart disease if you have abdominal obesity—that is, if you have a "big gut" or are "apple shaped." Add in insulin resistance, high cholesterol, high triglycerides and high blood pressure, and your risk jumps even higher. But don't get discouraged. Studies show that just 30 minutes of moderate exercise each day can make a positive health difference.

In addition to running, follow the Heart Association's Dietary Guidelines; they are very similar to the ones listed above, with the addition of eating fish twice a week. The complete list is in Chapter 1 (page 13).

Dementia

What is good for your heart is also good for your brain! As your body ages, your brain ages as well, as noted by the statistic that only 1% of 60-year-olds have dementia, but 40% of 90-year-olds do.

You can reduce your risk of developing dementia by eating a heart-healthy diet. This means, fuel your body with more fruits and vegetables, nuts, olive oil and fish—preferably 8 ounces of oily fish each week (i.e., a can of tuna and a serving of salmon).

Summary

If you want to live a long life, it might as well be a health-filled life. Running and making wise food choices will work synergistically to hopefully delay, if not prevent, the diseases of aging and help you reach that goal. Making the effort to eat closer to the earth, enjoy simple foods in their natural form, and eating even-sized meals on a regular schedule are steps you can take each day to help you stay on the road to longevity. Don't end up bed-ridden, wishing you had taken better care of your body.

Fish and Broccoli Soup

When good health is your wish, get hooked on fish and vegetables. This simple recipe is an easy way to enjoy both! For a heartier meal, add leftover cooked rice or pasta (shells, bow ties or other small shapes).

1 cup	(240 ml)	chicken broth, regular or low sodium (canned or from bouillon cubes)
$^1/_3$ lb	(150 g)	fish, preferably white such as cod, haddock, sole
1 cup	(150 g)	fresh or frozen broccoli, chopped
1 tablespoon	(15 g)	cornstarch mixed in
1 tablespoon	(15 ml)	water

Optional: $^3/_4$ cup (100 g) cooked rice or pasta; 1 teaspoon (5 ml) sesame oil.

1. Heat the chicken broth in a small saucepan.

2. Add the cut up fish and chopped broccoli, along with the sesame oil, if desired. Bring to a boil, and then turn down the heat.

3. Simmer for about 5 minutes or until the broccoli is tender-crisp and the fish is no longer translucent.

4. Stir in the cornstarch mixed with water to thicken the broth. (You can omit this step if you have no cornstarch handy.)

Yield:	1 serving
Nutrition Information:	
Total calories:	200
Carbohydrate:	15 g
Protein:	33 g
Fat:	1 g

SECTION II

Chapter 6
Carbohydrates: The Fundamental Fuel

As a runner, you need carbohydrates to fuel your muscles and feed your brain. You can consume carbs by eating fruits, vegetables, grains and any form of starch or sugar, be it banana, (brown) rice, pasta, potato, honey, sports drink, gum drops or even marshmallows. Obviously, you'll enhance your health if you choose carbs primarily from fruits, vegetables and whole grains. But the sugary foods do offer the "gas" that fuels your muscles. The sugars just fail to offer any health protective vitamins or minerals.

CARBS, PROTEIN, FATS AND FLUIDS—THE RIGHT BALANCE

Today, questions abound about the role of carbohydrates in the sports diet—as well as concerns about insulin (the hormone that helps store carbs in the muscles) and the glycemic effect of foods (that is, the rate a carbohydrate enters the blood stream). The purpose of this chapter is to address carbohydrate confusion and provide some clarity for runners who want to eat wisely for good health, high energy, weight control and top performance.

Q: Are carbs fattening? ... Should I eat less of them?

A: Carbohydrates are not inherently fattening. Excess calories are fattening. Excess calories of carbohydrates (bread, bagels and pasta) are actually less fattening than are excess calories of fat (butter, mayonnaise and frying oils) because the body has to spend calories to convert excess carbohydrates into body fat. In comparison, the body easily converts excess dietary fat into body fat. This means that if you are destined to be gluttonous but want to suffer the least amount of weight gain, you might want to indulge in (high carb) frozen yogurt instead of (high fat) gourmet ice cream. See Chapter 14 for more information about how to lose weight and have energy to exercise.

Q: If carbs aren't fattening, why do high protein diets "work"?

A: High protein diets seemingly "work" because?

1. The dieter loses water weight. Carbs hold water in the muscles. For each ounce of carbohydrate you stored as glycogen, your body simultaneously stores about three ounces of water. When you exercise, your body releases the water.

2. People eliminate calories when they stop eating carbohydrates. For example, you might eliminate not only the baked potato (200 calories) but also two pats of butter (100 calories) on top of the potato; this creates a calorie deficit.

3. Protein tends to be more satiating than carbohydrate. That is, protein and fat linger longer in the stomach than carbohydrate. Hence, having 200 calories of high protein eggs for breakfast will satiate you longer than 200 calories of high carb toast with jam. By curbing hunger, you have fewer urges to eat and can more easily restrict calories—that is, until you start to crave carbs and over-eat them. (You know the scene: "Last chance to eat bread before I go back on my diet, so I'd better eat the whole loaf now...")

The overwhelming reason why high protein diets do NOT work is people fail to stay on them forever. Remember: You should never start a food program you do not want to maintain for the rest of your life. Do you really want to never eat breads, potato or crackers ever again? Your better option is to learn how to manage carbs, not avoid them.

Q: Is there a difference between the carbs from starchy foods (like breads) vs. the carbs in fruits and vegetables or in candy?

A: As far as your muscles are concerned, there is no difference. You can carbo-load on jellybeans, bananas or brown rice; they are biochemically similar. Sugars and starches both offer the same amount of energy (4 calories per gram, or 16 calories per teaspoon) and both can get stored as glycogen in muscles or used for fuel by the brain (via the blood sugar).

The sugar in jellybeans is a simple compound, one or two molecules linked together. The starch in (brown) rice is a complex compound with hundreds to thousands of sugar molecules linked together. Sugars can convert into starches and starches can convert into sugars. For example, a green (not ripe) banana is starchy. A ripe banana becomes sweeter; in fruits, the starch converts into sugar. Peas are sweet when they are young. As they get older, they get starchier; in vegetables, the sugar converts into starch.

Grain foods (wheat, rice, corn and oats) also store their energy as complex strands of sugar molecules, a starch. The starch breaks down into individual sugar molecules (glucose) during digestion. Hence, your muscles don't care if you eat sugars or starches for fuel because they both digest into the same simple sugar: glucose.

The difference between sugars and starches comes in their nutritional value and impact on your health. Some sugars and starches are healthier than others. For example, the sugar in orange juice is accompanied by vitamin C, folate and potassium. The sugar in orange soda is void of vitamins and minerals; that's why it's described as "empty calories." The starch in whole wheat bread is accompanied by fiber and phytochemicals. The starch in white breads has lost many health protective nutrients during the refining process.

Q: Is white bread "poison"?

A: White bread offers lackluster nutrition, but it is not "poison" nor a "bad" food. White bread can be balanced into an overall wholesome diet (as can pasta and other foods made from refined while flour). That is, if you have whole grain Wheaties for breakfast and brown rice for dinner, your diet can healthfully accommodate a sandwich made on white bread for lunch. White breads and food made from refined flour tend to be enriched with B-vitamins, iron and folate— all important nutrients for runners. According to the US Dietary Guidelines, about half of your grain choices can appropriately be refined, enriched grains.

Q: Is sugar "evil"?

A: Sugar is fuel, not evil. While the sugar in oranges and other fruits is accompanied by important vitamins and minerals, the sugar in, let's say, jelly beans is void of nutritional value. In general, I suggest runners limit their refined sugar intake to about 10% of total calories. That's about 200 to 300 calories of sugar per day; 200 calories equates to a quart of Gatorade, two gels, 16 ounces of soda, or 10 jellybeans.

Most runners can handle sugar just fine. But for a few, sugar seems "evil" because it contributes to swings in blood sugar levels that can result in feeling lightheaded and shaky. If you are "sugar sensitive" and notice that sugar makes you feel poorly, choose sugar along with protein, such as jelly with peanut butter, apple with lowfat cheese, or fruit yogurt with almonds.

Q: Should I avoid sugar pre-exercise?

A: The best advice regarding pre-exercise sugar is for you to *avoid the desire for sugar* by having eaten appropriately prior to exercise. For example, if you crave sugar before an afternoon training run, you could have prevented the desire for sugary, quick-energy foods by having eaten a bigger breakfast and lunch. Sugar cravings can be a sign you have gotten too hungry.

Note that sugar taken right before and during exercise is unlikely to contribute to a hypoglycemic reaction because muscles quickly use the sugar without the need for extra insulin. This includes sports drinks, gels, sports beans, gummy candies and other popular sugary choices. See Chapter 10 for more advice about pre-exercise fueling.

"I never used to eat carbs before my runs, but I realized I was running out of energy and feeling lightheaded and dizzy. So I made my self eat something. I started with a handful of Cheerios, and worked my way up to a bowl of cereal. Now, my body is used to eating pre-run and I enjoy my runs a whole lot more!"

Meghan Downing, Providence, RI

Q: Should I choose foods based on their glycemic effect (that is, the rate at which they cause blood sugar to increase)?

A: No; the glycemic response to a food varies from person to person, as well as from meal to meal (depending on the combinations of foods you eat). You'll be better off experimenting with a variety of grains, fruits and vegetables to learn what food combinations settle well, satisfy your appetite and offer lasting energy.

Wholesome, fiber-rich fruits, vegetables, beans and whole grains are wise food choices not because they tend to have a low glycemic effect (that is, cause a slow rise in blood sugar) but because they are nutrient-dense, can curb your appetite and may even help with weight management.

Building Carb-based Meals

As a runner, you should eat carbohydrates as the foundation of each meal. This can mean cereal for breakfast, sandwiches made on hearty bread for lunch, and for dinner, a meal that includes a starch such as pasta, potato or rice. While you can get some carbs from fruits and veggies, most runners do not get enough carbs from these foods alone. Hence, they need the carb-boost from dinner starches such as pasta, rice and potato.

Summary

Carbohydrates should not be a source of confusion. To the contrary: wholesome carbs—fruits, vegetables and grains—clearly should be the foundation of your sports diet. And, if desired, refined carbs—soda , sugar, and sports drinks—can be consumed in moderation. As a runner, you may be unable to get adequate carbs from fruits and veggies to fuel your muscles, so be sure to include some pasta, potato, rice or other starch in your dinner menu. By "carbo-loading" every day, your muscles will have the fuel they need to train at their best, and this will help you improve quickly, feel good and enjoy your runs.

Pasta, Potato and Rice: Quick and Easy Menu Ideas

As a runner, you should enjoy some type of potato, rice, pasta or other starchy food as the foundation of each dinner. These starches supply the carbs you need to fuel your muscles. Here are some quick and easy ideas to add variety to your menus.

Quick and Easy Ideas for Pasta Toppings

When you are tired of the same old spaghetti sauce, straight from the jar, try one of these ideas for a change of pasta toppings:

- Salsa
- Salsa heated in the microwave, then mixed with cottage cheese
- Olive oil with red pepper flakes
- Italian salad dressing mixed with a little Dijon mustard
- (Low-fat) salad dressings of your choice with steamed vegetables
- Low-fat sour cream and Italian seasonings
- Steamed, chopped broccoli with Parmesan cheese
- Parmesan cheese and a sprinkling of herbs (basil, oregano, Italian seasonings)
- Chicken breast sautéed with oil, garlic, onion, and basil
- Chili with kidney beans, topped with low-fat cheese
- Lentil soup (thick)
- Spaghetti sauce with a spoonful of grape jelly (adds a "sweet 'n sour" taste)
- Spaghetti sauce with canned chicken or tuna, tofu cubes, canned beans, cottage cheese, ground beef or turkey (for protein)

Winning Recipes

Quick and Easy Ideas for Potato Toppings

When you don't know what to do with yet-another baked potato, try one of these ideas:

- Low-fat salad dressing
- Low-fat sour cream, chopped onion and grated low-fat cheddar cheese
- Cottage cheese and garlic powder
- Cottage cheese and salsa
- Milk mashed into the potato
- Plain yogurt
- Mustard or ketchup
- Mustard and Worcestershire sauce
- Vinegar and flavored vinegars
- Soy sauce
- Pesto
- Chopped chives and green onion
- Herbs, such as dill, parsley, chopped chives
- Steamed broccoli or other cooked vegetables
- Chopped jalapeño peppers
- Lentils or lentil soup
- Soup broth
- Applesauce

Quick and Easy Ideas for Rice

Here are a few rice suggestions for hungry runners.

Cook rice in:

- Chicken or beef broth
- A mixture of orange or apple juice and water
- Water with seasonings: cinnamon, soy sauce, oregano, curry, chili powder or whatever might nicely blend with the menu.

Top rice with:

- Leftover chili
- Low-fat or fat-free Italian dressing and mustard
- Toasted sesame seeds
- Steamed vegetables
- Chopped mushrooms and green peppers, either raw or sautéed
- Low-fat or fat-free sour cream, raisins, tuna and curry powder
- Raisins, cinnamon and applesauce

Chapter 7
Protein for Muscles

Between ads for protein supplements and hype about the Atkins Diet (that wrongly deems protein as slimming), many runners erringly believe protein should be the foundation of their sports diets. While you do need adequate protein, it should be an accompaniment to the carb-based meals that fuel your muscles. Smaller amounts of protein—about 10 to 15 percent of your calories—can adequately build and repair muscles, make red blood cells, enzymes and hormones, and allow hair and fingernails to grow. This translates into a little bit of protein at each meal.

How Much Protein Is Enough?

For a new runner, an adequate and safe protein intake is about 0.5 to 0.8 grams of protein per pound of body weight (1.0 to 1.6 g/kg). This is slightly more than a sedentary person needs (0.4 g protein/lb body weight; 0.8 g/kg). The typical female runner needs approximately 50 to 70 grams of protein per day, the typical male runner, 70 to 90 grams of protein. The following chart can help you calculate your protein needs.

How to Balance Your Protein Intake

If you wonder if you are eating too little (or too much) protein, you can estimate your daily protein needs by multiplying your weight (or a good weight for your body) by 0.5 to 0.75 grams of protein per pound (1.0 to 1.5 g protein/kg).

Weight in lbs (kg)	Protein (grams/day)
100 (45)	50-80
120 (55)	60-90
150 (68)	75-100
170 (77)	85-115

Use food labels and the following chart to calculate your protein intake. Pay close attention to portion sizes!

Approximate Protein Content of Some Commonly Eaten Foods

Animal Proteins	Protein (grams)
Beef, 4 oz, (120g) cooked*	32
Chicken breast, small 4 oz. cooked	32
Tuna, 1 can (6.5 ounces)	40
Meat, fish, poultry, 1 oz. (30 g) cooked	7-8
Egg, 1	7
Egg white, 1	3

*4 ounces cooked = size of a deck of cards / 4 ounces cooked = 5 to 6 ounces raw

Plant		Protein (g)
Lentils, beans,	1/2 cup (100 g)	7
Baked beans,	1/2 cup (130 g)	7
Peanut butter,	2 tablespoons (30 g)	8
Tofu,	1/4 cake firm (4 oz, 120 g)	8
Soy milk,	1 cup (240 ml)	7

Dairy Products		
Milk, yogurt,	1 cup (240 ml)	8
Cheese,	1 ounce (30 g)	8
Cheese,	1 slice American (2/3 oz; 20 g)	4
Cottage cheese,	1/3 cup (75 g)	8
Milk powder,	1/4 cup (30 g)	8

Breads, Cereals, Grains		
Bread, 1 slice	(30 g)	2
Cold cereal,	1 ounce (30 g)	2
Oatmeal,	1/3 cup dry (30 g), or 1 cup cooked	5
Rice,	1/3 cup dry (55 g), or 1 cup cooked	4
Pasta,	2 ounces dry (60 g), or 1 cup cooked	7

Starchy Vegetables		
Peas, carrots,	1/2 cup (80 g) cooked	2
Corn,	1/2 cup cooked (80 g)	2
Beets,	1/2 cup cooked (80)	2
Winter squash,	1/2 cup (100 g)	2
Potato,	1 small (125 g)	2

Fruits, Watery Vegetables
Negligible amounts of protein.
Most fruits and vegetables have only small amounts of protein. They may contribute a total of 5 to 10 grams protein per day, depending on how much you eat.

Vegetarian Runners

Some health-conscious runners have reduced their meat (and saturated fat) intake, with hopes of reducing their risk of heart disease. While this is a good idea, some of these non-meat eaters fail to add any plant proteins to their daily meals. They live on cereal, bagels, pasta, fruit and vegetables—and they end up with a protein-deficient diet.

If you prefer a plant-based diet, make sure you are addressing your overall protein needs. You need to consume a small amount of protein-containing plant food (soy milk, peanut butter, hummus, etc.) at each meal. Otherwise, you'll feel the results of a protein imbalance: chronic fatigue, anemia, lack of improvement, muscle wasting, and an overall run-down feeling.

"As a new runner and a vegetarian, I learned I had to pay attention to getting enough protein in my diet. Otherwise, I felt too weak to run."

Dave Moench, Auburn, WA

Quick and Easy Meatless Meals

Here a few ideas to help you with a meat-free diet that has adequate protein.

Breakfast:

Cold cereal (preferably iron-enriched, as noted on the label):
Top with (soy) milk or yogurt and sprinkled with a few nuts.

Oatmeal, oat bran, and other hot cereals:
Add peanut butter, almonds or other nuts, and/or powdered milk.

Toast, bagels:
Top with low-fat cheese, cottage cheese, hummus or peanut butter.

Snacks:

Assorted nuts
Almond butter on rice cakes or crackers
Yogurt (Note: Frozen yogurt has only 4 grams of protein per cup, as compared to 8 grams of protein in regular yogurt.)

Lunch and Dinner:

Salads:
Add tofu, chickpeas, three-bean salad, marinated kidney beans, cottage cheese, sunflower seeds, chopped nuts.

Protein-rich salad dressing:
Add salad seasonings to plain yogurt, or blenderized tofu or cottage cheese (diluted with milk or yogurt).

Spaghetti sauce:
Add diced tofu and/or canned, drained kidney beans. ▼

Pasta:
Choose protein-enriched pastas that offer 13 grams of protein per cup (140 g), as compared to 8 grams in regular pasta. Top with grated part-skim mozzarella cheese.

Potato:
Bake or microwave, then top with canned beans, baked beans or low-fat cottage cheese.

Hearty soups:
Choose lentil, split pea, bean and minestrone.

Hummus:
Enjoy hummus with pita or tortillas.

Cheese pizza:
A protein-rich fast food; half of a 12-inch pizza has about 40 grams of protein.

Beans

For vegetarian runners, beans are not only a good source of protein, but also of carbohydrates, B-vitamins (such as folate) and fiber. When added to an overall low-fat diet, they may help lower elevated blood cholesterol levels. (The problem with beans is flatulence; some runners become gas propelled!)

To add more beans to your sports diet:

- Sauté garlic and onions in a little oil; add canned, drained beans (whole or mashed); and heat together.
- Add beans to salads, spaghetti sauce, soups and stews for a protein booster.
- In a blender, mix black beans, salsa and cheese. Heat in the microwave and use as a dip or on top of tortillas or potatoes.

Red Meat

Red meats, such as beef and lamb, are indisputably excellent sources of high-quality protein as well as iron (prevents anemia) and zinc (helps with healing). These two minerals are important for optimal health and athletic performance. Yet, some new runners are a bit unsure if eating red meat is a positive addition to their sports diet. The answer is complex; you need to weigh nutrition facts, ethical concerns, personal values, environmental issues, and dedication to making appropriate food choices. The following information can help you decide if tucking two to four small (3—4 ounce) portions of red meat into your weekly meals might enhance the quality of your diet.

Meat and cholesterol: Meat, like chicken, fish and other animal products, contains cholesterol. Cholesterol is a part of animal cells; plant cells contain no cholesterol. Most animal proteins have similar cholesterol values: 70–80 milligrams of cholesterol per four ounce serving of red meat, poultry and fish.

Given that the American Heart Association recommends that healthy people with normal blood cholesterol levels eat less than 300 milligrams of cholesterol per day, small portions of red meat can certainly fit those requirements. The *saturated fat* in greasy hamburgers, pepperoni, juicy steaks and sausage are the bigger concern in terms of heart health (and weight). Better choices include London broil, extra-lean hamburger and top round roast beef.

Meat and iron: Adequate iron in your sports diet is important to prevent anemia. Without question, the iron in red meat is more easily absorbed than that in popular vegetarian sources of iron (e.g., beans, raisins and spinach) or in supplements. But any iron is better than no iron.

How to Boost Your Iron Intake

- The recommended intake for iron is 8 milligrams for men and 18 milligrams for women per day. Women have higher iron needs to replace the iron lost from menstrual bleeding. Women who are post-menopausal require only 8 milligrams of iron per day.
- Iron from animal products is absorbed better than that from plant products.
- A source of vitamin C at each meal enhances iron absorption.

Source		Iron (mg)
Animal Sources (best absorbed)		
Beef, 4 oz	(120 g) cooked	4
Pork, 4 oz	(120 g)	1
Chicken breast, 4 oz	(120 g)	1
Chicken leg, 4 oz	(120 g)	1.5
Salmon, 4 oz	(120 g)	1
Fruits		
Prunes, 5		1
Raisins, 1/3 cup	(45 g)	1
Vegetables		
Spinach, 1/2 cup	(100 g) cooked	3
Broccoli, 1 cup	(180 g) cooked	1
Beans		
Kidney, 1/2 cup	(130 g)	2.5
Tofu, 1/4 cake	(120 g)	2

▼

Grains		
Cereal, 100% iron fortified 1 oz	(30 g)	18
Spaghetti, 1 cup cooked	(140 g)	2
Bread, 1 oz (30 g) slice, enriched		1

Other		
Molasses, blackstrap,		
1 tablespoon	(15 g)	3.5
Wheat germ, $1/4$ cup	(30 g)	2

Meat and zinc: Zinc is important for healing both the minor damage that occurs with daily training as well as major injuries and ailments. It is best found in iron-rich foods (e.g., red meat). Diets deficient in iron may then also be deficient in zinc. Like iron, the zinc in animal products is absorbed better than that in vegetable foods or supplements.

How to Boost Your Zinc Intake

- The recommended intake for zinc is 8 milligrams for women and 11 milligrams for men per day.
- Animal foods, including seafood, are the best sources of zinc.

Animal Sources		Zinc (mg)
Beef, tenderloin, 4 ounces	(120 g)	7
Chicken leg, 4 ounces	(120 g)	3.5
Pork loin, 4 ounces	(120 g)	3
Chicken breast, 4 ounces	(120 g)	1
Cheese, 1 ounce	(30 g)	1
Milk, 1 cup	(240 ml)	1
Oysters, 6 medium	(3 oz; 90 g)	75 (!)
Tuna, 1 can	(6 oz; 170 g)	2
Clams, 9 small	(3 oz; 90 g)	1

Plant Sources		Zinc (mg)
Wheat germ, $1/4$ cup	(30 g)	3.5
Lentils, 1 cup	(200 g)	2.5
Almonds, 1 oz	(30 g)	1
Garbanzo beans, $1/2$ cup	(100 g)	1
Spinach, 1 cup	(200 g) cooked	0.7
Peanut butter, 1 tablespoon	(15 g)	0.5
Bread, 1 slice	(30 g), whole wheat	0.5

Why Chicken Has Light and Dark Meat

The white and dark meat in chicken (and turkey) is a handy example of the two kinds of muscle fibers that help you exercise:

- Fast-twitch fibers (white breast meat) are used for quick bursts of energy.
- Slow-twitch fibers (dark leg, thigh and wing meat) function best for endurance exercise.

Elite runners tend to have the right combination of both—a high proportion of slow-twitch fibers for the long run, but also enough fast-twitch fibers for the sprint to the finish.

Slow-twitch muscles, more so than fast-twitch, rely on fat for fuel. This is why dark meat contains more fat than the white meat. On the plus side, dark meat also contains more nutrients—iron, zinc, and B-vitamins, many of the same nutrients found in red meats.

Chicken, without skin, 4 oz (120) cooked	Calories	Fat (g)	Iron (mg)
Breast, white meat	180	4	1.2
Thigh, dark meat	235	12	1.5
Leg, dark meat	200	6	1.4

If you do not eat red meats, you might want to include more dark meat from chicken or turkey in your sports diet. For the small price of a few grams of fat, you'll get more nutritional value. If you want to cut back on fat, eliminate the skin—the fattiest part of poultry.

Get Hooked on Fish

Runners are not immune from heart disease! The protein in fish is rich in omega-3 fat, the good fat that protects against heart attacks and strokes. The American Heart Association (AHA) recommends eating two fish meals per week, particularly oily fish, such as trout, salmon, tuna, sardines and herring.

Eating fish comes with risks related to mercury and PCBs (polychlorinated biphenyls). The Food and Drug Administration (FDA) and the Environmental Protection Agency (EPA) advise women who may become pregnant or who currently are pregnant or breast feeding—and their young children—to avoid the fish highest in mercury (shark, swordfish, king mackerel/ono and tilefish). Large amounts of methyl mercury can harm an unborn or young child's developing nervous system, resulting in problems with IQ, attention, reading and memory. But everyone—including pregnant women—can safely enjoy up to twelve ounces (two or three fish meals) per week of low-mercury fish and shellfish: shrimp, salmon, pollock, catfish and canned light tuna.

The health benefits of eating fish generally far outweigh the risks. The trick to eating fish is to consume a variety of different fish, with a focus on the smaller fish. Each week, enjoy a meal with oily fish (salmon, blue fish) and another with low-mercury fish (pollock, sole). Be moderate, and you'll get hooked on good health.

Protein bars

When you are on the run and grabbing meals, a protein bar can be a convenient way to get hassle-free, lowfat protein. But because it is an engineered food, it lacks the wholesome goodness and yet-to-be-identified compounds that nature puts in all natural sources of protein. Most protein bars include protein from whey or casein (milk is about 20% whey, 80% casein), soy and/or egg—all of which are excellent sources of amino acids. Some of the bars are handy snacks; others are hefty enough to be a meal replacement. They fall into the category of "convenient" but not "necessary."

Summary

Lean meat is a nutrient-dense sports food. The fat in greasy meats, not the red meat itself, is the primary health culprit. Chicken and fish are lower fat alternatives, with fish being the healthiest choice of all. If you prefer a vegetarian diet, just be sure to have a protein-rich food with each meal. Vegetarians who simply eliminate meat and make no effort to include alternate plant sources of protein, iron and zinc can suffer from dietary deficiencies that hurt their sports performance. Protein bars can be a handy "emergency food" when you are eating on the run and your protein needs would otherwise be neglected.

Recipe for Success: Baked Chicken with Mustard

Chicken has less saturated fat than many cuts of red meat; hence it can be a good alternative for dinner. But if you are tired of eating yet another boring chicken breast, here is a simple recipe to spice it up.

1 6-ounce	(150 g)	chicken breast, skinned
1-2 teaspoons	(5-10 ml)	prepared mustard
2 teaspoons	(10 g)	grated Parmesan cheese

1. Place the chicken in a nonstick pan (or a pan lined with aluminum foil, for easier clean-up).

2. Brush the chicken with mustard; sprinkle with Parmesan cheese.

3. Bake uncovered at 350°F (175°F) for 20 to 30 minutes, or until the juices run clear when poked with a fork.

Yield:	one serving
Nutrition Information:	
Total calories:	190
Calories per serving:	190
Carbohydrate:	trace
Protein:	26 g
Fat:	10 g

Other suggestions are:

- Spread with honey and sprinkle with curry powder
- Marinate for an hour or overnight in Italian dressing
- Spread with honey mustard

You can't cook chicken much simpler than this and still have it taste good enough for a company dinner! These recipes also work well with fish.

Winning Recipe

Chapter 8
Fat—The Right Kind for Your Sports Diet

Eat fat, get fat. Eat fat, clog your arteries. Eat fat, have a heart attack. Eat fat, run slow. I'm sure you've heard this anti-fat chatter. While there is an element of truth in some of these statements, there is also room for more education. Let's take a look at the whole picture.

While dietary fat used to be considered bad, we now know that all fats are not created equal. The hard, saturated fat in beef, butter and cheese is the "bad" fat, as is the trans- (partially hydrogenated) fat in commercially baked goods. The soft, liquid polyunsaturated and monounsaturated fats in fish, olives, peanut butter, and nuts are the "good" fats, essential for overall good health. Hence, there's no need to avoid all fat like the plague.

Olive oil, for example, is health-protective; it is the foundation of the acclaimed heart-healthy Mediterranean Diet. For centuries, native Italians and Greeks have enjoyed good health and a 40-percent-fat diet. In general, I recommend that healthy runners target a sports diet with about 25 percent of the calories from (primarily healthful) fat.

How does 25 percent fat translate into food? Let's say you have 1,800 calories a day in your calorie budget (this would be a reducing diet for most female runners):

.25 x 1,800 total calories = 450 calories a day of fat.

Because there are 9 calories per gram of fat, divide 450 calories by 9:

450 calories / 9 calories per gram = 50 grams of fat in your daily fat budget.

A 25-percent-fat diet includes a reasonable amount of fat and lets you enjoy a little fat at each meal. Preferably, you'll choose fat that has positive health value such as olive oil, salmon and other oily fish, all-natural peanut butter, nuts and tuna with light mayonnaise. But, if you do have the occasional hankering for a big burger with 25 grams of fat and 500 calories, simply fit it into your day's fat and calorie budget *and balance the rest of the day's meals*. (Refer to Chapter 13 to determine your calorie needs.)

"I used to suffer through fat-free cheese, but it just doesn't taste good. I'm now enjoying low-fat cheese, and am far happier!"

Karin Daisy, Taunton, MA

Fat Guidelines

The following guidelines can help you appropriately budget fat into your food plan.

Calories per day	Fat grams per day (for 25-percent-fat diet)
1,600	45
1,800	50
2,000	55
2,200	60
2,400	65

Fat Content of Some Common Foods

Food			Serving size	Fat (grams)	Calories
Dairy products					
Milk,	whole	(3.5% fat)	1 cup (240 ml)	8	150
	reduced-fat	(2% fat)	"	5	120
	low-fat	(1% fat)	"	2	100
	fat-free	(0% fat)	"	--	80
Cheese					
Cheddar			1 oz. (30 g)	9	110
	reduced-fat		"	5	90
mozzarella, part-skim		"		5	80
cottage cheese		(4% fat)	1/2 cup (120 g)	5	120
	low-fat	(2% fat)	"	2	90
Cream cheese			1 oz. (2 tbsp/30 g)	10	100
	light		"	5	60
Ice cream,	gourmet		1/2 cup (100 g)	15	250
	standard		" (80 g)	8	150
	light		" (70 g)	3	110

Food			Serving size	Fat (grams)	Calories
Frozen yogurt,		low-fat	" (70 g)	2	120
		fat-free	" (90 g)	--	100
Animal proteins					
Beef,	regular hamburger		4 oz. cooked (120 g)	24	330
	flank steak		"	12	235
	eye of round		"	6	200
Chicken,	breast, no skin		4 oz. cooked (120 g)	5	200
	thigh, no skin		"	11	235
Fish,	haddock		4 oz. cooked (120 g)	1	125
	swordfish		"	6	175
Vegetable proteins					
Beans,	kidney		$^{1}/_{2}$ cup cooked (100 g)	--	110
Lentils			"	--	110
Tofu			4 oz. (120 g)	5	90
Peanut butter			1 tbsp. (15 g)	8	95
Fats					
Butter			1 tbsp (15 g)	11	100
Margarine			"	11	100
Oil, olive			"	13	120
Mayonnaise			"	11	100
Grains					
Bread,	whole wheat		1 large slice (30 g)	1	90
Crackers,	Saltines		5	2	60
	Ritz		4	4	70
	Rice cakes		1	--	35

Food	Serving size	Fat (grams)	Calories
Cereal, shredded wheat	1 oz. (2/3 cup/ 30 g))	--	90
granola	1 oz. (1/4 cup/ 30 g))	6	130
oatmeal	1 oz. (1/3 cup/ 30 g) dry	2	100
Spaghetti, plain	2 oz. dry (1 cup cooked; 140 g))	1	210
Rice	2 oz. dry (1 cup cooked; 160 g))	--	200
Fast foods			
Big Mac	1	30	560
Egg McMuffin	1	12	300
French fries	small	13	250
KFC Fried chicken breast	1	19	380
Pizza, cheese	1 slice large	10 – 13	250
Snacks, Treats			
Cookie, Chips Ahoy	1 (1/2 oz; 15 g)	2	50
Fig Newton	1 (1/2 oz; 15 g)	1	60
Brownie, from mix	1 small	5	140
Graham crackers	2 squares	1	60
Potato chips	1 oz. (about 18 chips)	9	150
Pretzels	1 oz. (30 g)	1	110
Milky Way	1.75 oz. bar (50g)	8	220
M&Ms w/ peanuts	1.75 oz. (50 g) bag	13	250
Reese's Peanut Butter Cups	1.6 oz. (2 cups/ 45 g)	15	280
Fruits and Vegetables			
most varieties		negligible fat	

Fear of Fat

Without question, fat imparts a tempting taste, texture and aroma and helps make food taste great. That's why fatty foods can be hard to resist and are enjoyed to excess. Although excess fat-calories can easily turn into body fat, note the "eat fat, get fat" theory is false. Many active people eat appropriate amounts of fat and stay thin. They simply don't overeat calories.

If you obsess about every gram of fat to the extent you have a fat phobia, your fear of fat may be exaggerated! A little fat can actually aid in weight reduction because it takes longer to empty from the stomach—and offers that nice feeling of being satisfied after a meal. For example, you may have less desire to keep munching on, let's say, yet-another rice cake if you start by eating a rice cake with a little peanut butter.

As a runner, you want to include a little fat in each meal to not only help absorb certain vitamins but also to enhance performance. Runners who boosted their intake of healthful fat from 17% of calories to 30% of calories were not only able to run longer but also had less inflammation afterwards. Fat is certainly NOT a four-letter word!

Summary
Runners who include some fat in their daily training diet perform better than those who try to exclude fat. Obviously, choosing more of the healthful fat— olive oil, canola oil, nuts, peanut butter, salmon—is preferable to loading up on the fat from buttery cookies, greasy burgers and gourmet ice cream. But all fat eaten in moderation can be balanced into an overall healthful sports diet.

Sautéed Spinach with Garlic

Spinach, like all deeply colored vegetables, is nutrient-rich. By sautéing the spinach in a little olive oil, you retain more of the nutrients than if you were to cook it with water. Yes, you add a few more (health protective) calories, but also more flavor.

Be creative with this recipe; it works with a multitude of vegetables!

1 pound	(450 g)	fresh spinach
1 tablespoon	(15 ml)	olive oil
1 clove garlic, crushed or $^{1}/_{2}$ teaspoon (1-2 g) garlic powder		

1. Wash the spinach and remove the tough stems. Drain well.

2. In a skillet, heat the oil. Add the garlic and sauté for 1 to 2 minutes. Add the spinach and stir to coat. Cover and cook for 1 minute over medium-high heat.

3. Uncover and stir gently. Cook 1 to 2 more minutes.

Yield:	3 servings
Nutritional Information:	
Total calories:	210
Calories per serving:	70
Carbohydrate	5 g
Protein:	4 g
Fat:	4 g

Chapter 9
Fluids, Water and Sports Drinks

Preventing dehydration is an important part of your running program. As a new runner, you are unlikely to be become dehydrated because you will not be exercising for miles and miles (yet). However, if you are overweight and lugging around a lot of excess body fat, you might sweat heavily and lose significant amounts of fluid.

While you don't have to replace every drop of sweat, your goal should be to limit sweat loss to 2% of your body weight (3 lbs/1.5 kg for a 150 lb/68 kg person). Your heart rate increases by 3 to 5 beats per minute for every 1% of body weight loss. Hence, with increasing sweat losses, exercise feels harder; you'll enjoy it less, and you'll run slower. In extreme cases, becoming dehydrated can contribute to medical problems.

If you replace fluid losses poorly during training and are chronically dehydrated, you'll tend to experience needless fatigue and lethargy. Don't let that happen! You can tell if you are well hydrated by monitoring your urine:
- You should urinate frequently (every 2 to 4 hours) throughout the day.
- The urine should be clear and of significant quantity.
- Your morning urine should not be dark and concentrated. (See the Urine Color Chart.)

Urine Color Chart

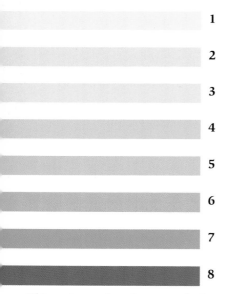

This urine color chart can help you determine if you have been consuming enough fluids to stay well hydrated. If your urine is darker than 3, drink more!

Reprint permission granted by L. Armstrong PhD

The Association of International Marathon Directors recommends you drink according to thirst. Thirst is a clear signal your body needs fluids. Or, you can follow the advice of the American College of Sports Medicine and learn your sweat rate so you can drink enough to match your sweat loss.

To determine how much you should drink during exercise, weigh yourself (without clothes) before and after a half-hour of running. If you have lost one pound (16 ounces; 450 ml) in 30 minutes, you've lost one pint (16 ounces; 450 ml) of sweat, and should plan to drink accordingly during the next exercise session—at least 8 ounces (225 ml) every fifteen minutes.

If you weigh 150 pounds (68 kg), try not to lose more than 3 pounds (1.5 kg) of sweat during a workout. Practice drinking fluids during training, as a means to teach your stomach to comfortably accommodate the fluids. Your body can turn water into sweat in about 10 minutes, so keep drinking, even towards the end of a long run.

"I experimented a lot with hydration. I now know how much to drink before and during runs so I don't have to urinate during the run, but have to urinate within 20 minutes of finishing. I like knowing I have consumed enough to replace what I lost in sweat."

Paula Sue Russell, Findlay, OH

"In the summer, before my long runs, I drive along the course and hide water bottles in the shrubs and behind telephone poles. Most of the time, the water is there when I run by and need a drink."

Amy Singer, Seattle

Running in the Heat

When running in the heat, pay attention to your training buddies and also listen to your own body. If you notice that you or your buddies feel light-headed, dizzy, nauseous, clumsy, uncoordinated, confused, irrational, have stopped sweating, or have ashen gray pale skin, stop! Those are all symptoms of heat illness.

Here's what to do:
- lay down in a shady or cool place
- raise legs and hips to improve blood pressure
- remove excess clothing
- cool off by wetting the skin liberally and fanning vigorously
- apply ice pack to groin, armpits and neck
- drink cool water (if conscious)

Water or Sports Drinks?

Water is an adequate fluid replacer during runs that last less than 60 minutes. Sports drinks are helpful during training sessions that last longer than 60 to 90 minutes. As you are able to run for longer distances, you'll discover you perform better and feel better if you consume a sports drink during the long runs. A sports drink provides:

- small amounts of *carbohydrates* to fuel your mind and muscles.
- *sodium* to enhance water absorption and retention.
- *water* to replace sweat loss.

Comparing Common Fluid Replacers

Beverage (8 oz.)	Calories	Sodium (mg)	Potassium (mg)
Propel	10	35	0
Gatorade	50	110	30
Gatorade Endurance	50	200	90
PowerAde	70	55	30
Cola	100	5	--
Beer	100	12	60
Orange juice	110	2	475
Cranapple juice	175	5	70
Fruit yogurt	250	150	465
Possible losses in 2 hours	1,000	1,000	180

With the multitude of sports drinks on the market, you may feel confused about what's best to drink, and wonder which ones are better than the others. The bottom line is you should choose the drink that tastes best to you; there are no significant advantages to one over the other. The most important point is to *drink enough*. For more information, see Chapter 11, Foods and Fluids During Runs Longer than an Hour.

Sodium Replacement

When you sweat, you lose sodium, an electrolyte (electrically charged particle) that helps maintain proper water balance in your tissues. Most novice runners don't have to worry about replacing sodium during exercise because the losses are generally too small to cause a deficit that will hurt performance and/or health.

But, *if you will be exercising for more than four hours* (unlikely for new runners!), sodium loss can become problematic, particularly if you are drinking only water during that time. Drinking excessive water dilutes the sodium outside the cells; this causes too much water to seep into cells and the cells swell—including the cells in the brain. Symptoms that progressively appear include feeling weak, groggy, nauseous and incoherent; ultimately leading to stumbling, seizures, coma and death. Hence, your best bet during extended exercise is to choose sports drinks and foods that contain sodium.

The rule of thumb is to add extra salt to your diet if you have lost more than four to six pounds of sweat (3- to 4-percent of your body weight pre- to post-exercise). Salty sweaters (who end up with a crust of salt on their skin after a hard workout) and heavy sweaters (who lose more than 2 lbs/ 1 kg sweat per hour) should pay close attention to their sodium intake—particularly if you are not acclimatized to running in the heat. Endurance sports drinks (with more sodium than the standard sports drink), pretzels, V-8 juice, chicken broth, salt-packets (from a restaurant) and pickles are just a few ways to boost sodium intake.

Sodium in Commonly Eaten Foods

In general, most novice runners consume adequate sodium, even without adding salt to their food. But, if you crave salt, you should eat it. Salt cravings signal that your body wants salt. If you hanker for some pretzels or salty foods after a long run, eat them!

Here are some common sources of sodium that can easily replace the estimated 500 milligrams of sodium you might lose in an hour of running.

Food	Sodium (mg)
Bread, 1 slice	150
Cheese, 1 oz (30 g)	220
Egg, 1	60
Yogurt, 8 oz/240 ml	125
Broth, canned 8 oz/240 ml	900
Pizza, 2 slices	1,200
Whopper	1,450

How to Keep Your Cool

Here's a short true-false quiz to test your knowledge about fluid replacement and help you survive the heat in good health and with high energy.

Drinking cold water during running will cool you off.
True (but by a small margin). Although drinking cold water will cool you off slightly more than warmer water, the difference is small. That's because the water

quickly warms to body temperature. The more important concern is quantity. Any fluid of any temperature is better than no fluid.

Soda is a poor choice during exercise because the carbon dioxide in the bubbles will slow you down.
False. Historically, runners were always warned to "de-fizz" carbonated beverages taken during exercise, fearing that the carbonation would hurt performance. Not the case. No studies comparing carbonated and non-carbonated soft drinks suggest bubbles will slow you down or result in stomach discomfort.

Beer is an appropriate recovery fluid.
False. Although beer is a popular post-exercise recovery drink, its alcohol content has both a dehydrating and depressant effect. If you drink beer on an empty stomach (as commonly happens post-race), you can quickly negate the pleasurable "natural high" that you would otherwise enjoy. Wise beer-drinkers first have 1 to 2 glasses of water and eat some carbohydrate-rich foods (e.g., pretzels, pizza, crackers) and then, if desired, enjoy a beer or two in moderation.

Beverages are low in calories and are "free foods" for dieters.
False. The calories you drink are more likely to contribute to fat gain than calories you chew. That's because liquid calories are less filling and don't contribute much to satiety (that nice feeling of having been fed). Think of a regular soda as a sugary treat, not as a standard beverage.

Homemade Sports Drink

The main ingredients in commercial fluid replacers are:

Sugar.   Sports drinks are 5 to 7 percent sugar; they contain about 12 grams of carbohydrate (50 calories) per 8 ounces; this is equal to 3 teaspoons (8 g) of sugar per cup.

Sodium.   Sports drinks contain 50 to 110 milligrams of sodium per 8 ounces; this is equal to $^1/_8$ teaspoon or 1 pinch of salt per cup.

This recipe comes close enough. Give it a try if you want a low-cost fluid replacer.

3 teaspoons	(12 g)	sugar
$^1/_4$ teaspoon	(1 g)	salt
$^1/_4$ cup	(60 ml)	orange juice
3 $^1/_2$ cups	(840 ml)	cold water

1. In the bottom of a 1 quart (1 liter) bottle, dissolve the sugar in a little bit of hot water.

2. Add the salt and juice.

3. Add the cold water.

4. Quench that thirst!

YIELD:	1 quart or 4 8-oz. servings (~1 liter; 4 240-ml servings)

Nutrition Information:

Total calories:	200
Calories per serving:	50
Carbohydrate	12 g
Protein	0 g
Fat	0 g
Sodium	110 mg
Potassium	30 mg

SECTION III

Chapter 10
Fueling Before You Run

One of the biggest mistakes made by novice runners—particularly those who want to lose weight—is to train on empty. They think this will help them lose fat and run faster. Wrong! Just as your car works best with gas in its tank, your body works best when it has been appropriately fueled. You can lose weight at other times of the day, but don't run on empty! (For weight reduction information, please read Chapter 14).

SPORTS NUTRITION—
THE RIGHT FOODS AT THE RIGHT TIMES

Pre-exercise food contributes to stamina and endurance. If you have always abstained from eating within the hour or two before you exercise just because you thought you should run with an empty stomach, think again. I encourage you to try a light snack. You might be pleasantly surprised by the benefits—particularly if you will be running for more than a few miles. You will enjoy the miles more when you are adequately fueled.

New (and experienced) runners commonly avoid pre-exercise food because for them, it causes intestinal distress. An estimated 25 to 30 percent of runners experience abdominal cramps, diarrhea and/or the need for pit stops during or immediately after running. Running jostles the stomach, and the food sometimes "talks back." If that's your case, you'll want to train your intestinal track to tolerate little bits of food—a saltine, a pretzel—and gradually increase to 100 to 300 calories of a pre-run snack.

Because eating ability and food preferences vary in relation to when, how long and how hard you run, if you plan to build up to more than an hour of running you should *practice* pre-exercise eating and remember that you are training your intestinal track, not just your heart, lungs and muscles.

Please consider the following pre-exercise eating recommendations as possible experiments, and learn through trial and error:

- what foods work best for your body.
- when you should eat them.
- what amounts are appropriate.

You are an experiment of one and only *you* can best determine what works best for your body.

"When I first started to run, I frequently struggled with an upset stomach from eating too close to my runs. The stomach issues resolved when I started running two to three hours after a meal."

Jill Roberts, Tampa, FL

If you run at a pace that you can comfortably maintain for more than 30 minutes, your body can both run and digest food at the same time. At this comfortable training pace, the blood flow to your stomach is 60 to 70 percent of normal—adequate to maintain normal digestion processes. But the harder you run, the less likely you will want to eat, and the more likely you will need to allow more digestion time between eating and exercising. Fast runners may feel nauseated at even the thought of pre-exercise food, while slow walkers appreciate the added energy.

If you are doing intense sprinting, your stomach essentially shuts down and gets only about 20 percent of its normal blood flow. This slows the digestion process so that any pre-exercise food will jostle along for the ride, and possibly "talk back." It may feel uncomfortable and cause indigestion or heartburn. Hence, you want to allow extra digestion time prior to a hard workout.

Five Benefits of Pre-exercise Fueling

If you are in the experimental stage of developing your pre-exercise food plan for various intensities of runs, the following information provides some helpful facts about the benefits of pre-exercise food. This information can help you as your runs get longer and longer; that's when the right combination of food and fluids will make or break your ability to complete the distance comfortably.

1. *Pre-exercise food helps prevent low blood sugar.* The carbohydrates in your pre-exercise snack are important because they fuel not only your muscles but also your mind. Why suffer with light-headedness, needless fatigue, irritability and inability to concentrate when you can prevent these symptoms of hypoglycemia? Adequate pre-run carbohydrates help you think clearly; the carbs digest into sugar and travel via the bloodstream to provide fuel for your brain.

Some sugar also gets stored in your liver, and gets released into the blood stream to maintain a normal blood sugar level. If you have low blood sugar due to low liver glycogen (as happens overnight, or in the afternoon if you fail to eat enough breakfast and lunch), your brain will be left unfed. You will feel tired, unable to concentrate on the task at hand, and will think you've "hit the wall." This is needless.

Some morning runners exercise without first eating, yet they report they feel fine and enjoy their runs. They have likely eaten a big dinner the night before and/or have done serious late-night snacking that bolsters their liver glycogen stores; this reduces their need for a morning energizer. This pattern is not bad or wrong, as long as it works well for them. (In general, runners who do most of their eating at the end of the day tend to have more body fat than those who fuel adequately during the day. See Chapter 14 for more information on weight management.)

2. *Pre-exercise food helps settle the stomach, absorbs some of the gastric juices and abates hunger feelings.*

The caloric density of a snack or meal affects the rate at which the food leaves your stomach. This explains why you can exercise comfortably soon after snacking on a few crackers or a piece of fruit, but you are better off waiting three or four hours after eating a heartier meal. The general pre-exercise "rule of thumb" is to allow:

- 3–4 hours for a large meal to digest
- 2–3 hours for a smaller meal
- 1–2 hours for a blended or liquid meal
- less than an hour for a small snack, as tolerated

3. *Pre-exercise food fuels the muscles.* The snack you eat even an hour before you run gets digested into glucose and burned for energy. For example, one study showed that runners who ate 400 calories of sugar three hours before an easy four-hour run burned about 70 percent of the sugar. If you have trouble with solid pre-exercise foods

300-calorie Pre-run Snack Suggestions

According to research, you might be able to increase your stamina by as much as 18 percent if you take in 0.5 grams of carbohydrate per pound of body weight (or 1 gram per kilogram) per hour of endurance exercise. For example, if you weigh 150 pounds, you should target about 75 grams of carbohydrates (300 calories) per hour. This could be:

- six 8-ounce glasses of a sports drink (50 calories per 8 ounces)
- four cups of sports drink and a banana
- two cups of sports drink plus a sports bar (plus extra water)
- five fig cookies plus water

This is more calories than many runners voluntarily consume during long runs. Hence, you need to practice programmed eating and drinking. Then, on the day of an event, you will know what and how much you can tolerate, as well as how you can comfortably carry the sports snacks.

(i.e., banana, bagel), you might want to experiment with liquids, such as a fruit smoothie or a canned liquid meal such as Boost.

In general, carbohydrates are digested more easily than fatty foods. Low-fat foods and meals (such as those listed in the sidebar, *High Carbohydrate Meal Suggestions*) tend to digest easily and settle well. In comparison, high-fat-bacon-and-fried-egg breakfasts, greasy hamburgers, tuna subs loaded with mayonnaise and grilled cheese sandwiches have been known to settle heavily and feel uncomfortable. Too much fat slows digestion, so the meal lingers longer in the stomach and may contribute to a weighed-down feeling. A little fat, however, such as in a slice of lowfat cheese on toast, a teaspoon of peanut butter on a bagel, or the fat in some brands of sports bars, can be appropriate. It provides both sustained energy and satiety during long runs.

> **High Carbohydrate Meal Suggestions**
>
> Some high-carbohydrate meal suggestions that keep your muscles well fueled include tried-and-true foods such as:
>
> | | |
> |---|---|
> | Breakfast: | cold cereals, oatmeal and other hot cereals, bagels, English muffins, pancakes, French toast with syrup, jam, honey, fruit, juice |
> | Lunch: | sandwiches (with the bread being the "meat" of the sandwich), fruit, thick-crust pizza, hearty broth-based soups with noodles or rice |
> | Dinner: | pasta, potato or rice entrées; veggies, breads, juice, fruit |
> | Snacks: | flavored yogurt, pretzels, crackers, fig bars, frozen yogurt, dry cereal, leftover pasta, zwieback, energy bars, simple biscuit-type cookies, animal crackers, canned and fresh fruits, juice |

4. *Pre-exercise beverages provide fluids to fully hydrate your body.* By drinking diluted juice or sports drinks before you exercise, you can optimize your fluid intake, as well as boost your carbohydrate and energy intake. The best pre-exercise fluid choices include water, sports drinks, diluted juices and even coffee or tea if you want a caffeine-boost.

5. *Pre-exercise food can pacify your mind with the knowledge that your body is well fueled.* Pre-exercise food has great psychological value. If you firmly believe that a specific food or meal will enhance your performance, then it probably will. Your mind has a powerful effect on your body's ability to

perform at its best. If you do have a "magic food" that assures athletic excellence, you should take special care to be sure this food or meal is available prior to the race.

"When I first started running, I wouldn't eat anything beforehand; I ended up being hungry and tired at the end. I've learned that eating just a little something—even RIGHT before leaving—such as two Fig Newtons or a piece of dry whole wheat toast, helps keep my energy up throughout the run. And if I keep it light, I don't have any stomach issues at all."

Becky Downie, Seattle, WA

Summary

Whether you are a jogger or a runner, pre-exercise food will help you better enjoy your training program. Just as you put gas in your car before you take it for a drive, you should put 100 to 300 calories of carbohydrate-rich food in your body within the hour before you exercise. You may need to train our intestinal track to tolerate this fuel, just like you are training your heart, lungs and muscles to go the distance. Granted, each runner is an experiment of one, and some runners can tolerate food better than others. That's why you need to experiment to determine what pre-exercise menu works best for you.

Reprinted with permission from Nancy Clark's Sports Nutrition Guidebook, Fourth Edition (Human Kinetics, 2008)

Peanutty Energy Bar

This prizewinning National Peanut Board recipe offers a yummy alternative to commercial energy bars. The bars are perfect for a satisfying afternoon snack to fuel you for a training run. The 9 grams of fat in each energy bar are from peanuts and sunflower seeds—health protective and a positive addition to a sports diet.

For variety, you can make this recipe with cashews and cashew butter and/or add a variety of dried fruits (cranberries, cherries and dates).

$^1/_2$ cup	(75 g)	salted dry-roasted peanuts
$^1/_2$ cup	(75 g)	roasted sunflower seed kernels or use more peanuts or other nuts
$^1/_2$ cup	(75 g)	raisins or other dried fruit
2 cups	(180 g)	uncooked oatmeal, old-fashioned or instant
2 cups	(180 g)	toasted rice cereal, such as Rice Krispies
$^1/_2$ cup	(120 g)	peanut butter, crunchy or creamy
$^1/_2$ cup	(90 g)	packed brown sugar
$^1/_2$ cup	(120 ml)	light corn syrup
1 teaspoon	(15 ml)	vanilla

Optional: $^1/_4$ cup (25 g) toasted wheat germ

1. In a large bowl, mix together the peanuts, sunflower seeds, raisins, oatmeal, and toasted rice cereal (and wheat germ). Set aside.
2. In a medium microwaveable bowl, combine the peanut butter, brown sugar and corn syrup. Microwave on high for 2 minutes. Add vanilla and stir until blended.
3. Pour the peanut butter mixture over the dry ingredients and stir until coated.
4. For squares, spoon the mixture into an 8 x 8-inch (20 x 20 x 5-cm) pan coated with cooking spray; for bars spoon it into a 9 x 13-inch (33 x 23 x 5-cm) pan. Press down firmly. (It helps to coat your fingers with margarine, oil or cooking spray.)
5. Let stand for about an hour, and then cut into squares or bars.

Yield:	16 squares or bars
Nutrition Information:	
Total calories:	3,600
Calories per serving:	225
Carbohydrate	30 g
Protein	6 g
Fat	9 g

Winning Recipe

Chapter 11
Foods and Fluids During Runs
Longer than an Hour

As a new runner, you are likely building up to 30 or 45 minutes of running, and maybe even an hour. What you eat before you run should carry you for that relatively short distance. But once you start running for more than 60 to 90 minutes, you should consume fuel *during* the run. If a marathon is in your future, you certainly need to learn what types of foods and fluids your body tolerates best during training runs. As I have mentioned before, the purpose of long training runs is to not only train your heart, lungs and muscles, but also to train your intestinal tract so you can keep yourself well fueled and hydrated. By doing so, you'll delay fatigue and prevent dehydration without discomfort and undesired pit stops.

More precisely, your goals during long runs are to:
1) Drink the right amount of fluid to prevent dehydration—and overhydration.
2) Consume enough carbs to prevent hypoglycemia (low blood sugar).

You can succeed at meeting these goals by drinking carbohydrate-containing fluids (such as a sports drink) or by combining water with solid foods (water + energy bar). You'll rarely see elite runners consuming more than a sports drink, but slower runners can do well with a variety of fluids and foods that they have used during training.

"I am a 'salty sweater' who had been struggling during my long runs—until I started taking with me twizzlers, pretzels and Gatorade (with an extra dash of salt). I now feel like a million bucks— even after a 14 miler."

Amanda Sherwin, Scotch Plains, NJ

Creating a Fueling Plan for Extended Exercise

During long training runs, be sure to drink every 15 to 20 minutes. Remember, you want to *prevent* dehydration. Don't let yourself get too thirsty. By drinking on a schedule—let's say, a target of about 4-8 ounces (120-240 ml), that's 4-8 gulps, of water or sports drink every 15 to 20 minutes—you can minimize dehydration, maximize your performance and reduce your recovery time.

As I wrote about in Chapter 9, learning your sweat rate helps you determine how much to drink and is important information, particularly if you sweat heavily. Be certain you make the effort to weigh yourself before and after a one-hour run so you'll know how much sweat you lose (and need to replace); one pound sweat = one pound of water lost (16 ounces; 480 g).

Within the first half-hour of your run, start drinking so you can maintain adequate hydration; once you are dehydrated, you won't catch up. Losing only 2 percent of your body weight (3 pounds for a 150-pound person; 1.4 kg for a 70 kg person) from sweating hurts your performance and upsets your ability to regulate your body temperature. (Refer to Chapter 9 for more details.) To keep hydrated:

- If you are training with a group, take advantage of the water stations your coach has set up along the route.
- If you are training by yourself, set up your own water stops. This means planning a route that includes adequate water fountains, or driving the route before your run/walk and placing bottles filled with water or sports drinks in strategic locations.
- Take fluids with you. Some marathoners prefer to run with a Camelback (a water bladder that straps to the back) or other portable water system.
- If you are in a race, check the website so you know in advance the location of each water station. If there is a water station every mile, you might want to drink at every other station (every 15 to 20 minutes) or according to thirst.

Yes, you should drink according to a schedule, but you should also pay attention to thirst. Don't force fluids. Drinking too much fluid to the point you feel the excess water sloshing around in your stomach causes problems—nausea, if not hyponatremia (low blood sodium). The immediate solution is to stop drinking for a while. The long-term solution is to practice drinking during training, so your body can adapt to the appropriate fluid intake.

You will feel happier and more energetic if you can replace not only water but also carbohydrates while running. These carbohydrates help to maintain a normal blood sugar level as well as provide a

Popular Snacks During a Long Run

A plethora of commercial sports snacks are available for long distance runners, yet "real foods" can work just as well. Experiment with a variety of textures (soft, hard, dry, moist) and flavors (sweet, sour, salty), knowing that tastes change as you become tired.

Solids:	Liquids:
Dried fruit	Diluted, defizzed cola
Energy bar	Sports drinks
Bagel	Iced tea with honey
Tootsie Rolls	Diluted juice
Hard candies	Iced coffee with sugar
Mini Chocolate bars	Go-Gurt (squeeze-pack yogurt)
Gummy candies	Honey sticks
Jellybeans	Gels
Sugar cookies	Water (with solid food)
Pretzels	Broth (for salt)
Banana	Meal-in-a-can (Boost, Ensure)

source of energy for muscles—and help you avoid hitting "the wall." The carbs you consume during a long will also help keep you in good spirits. Some runners become moody, irritable, and irrational towards the end of a long run. Training partners can become either the best of friends or the worst of enemies!

"Spending a lot of money on sports bars is not necessary. Yeah, some of them taste good and they are convenient, but there are cheaper foods out there—bananas, peanut butter on crackers, even PopTarts."

Liz Reichman, San Antonio, TX

Fuel Suggestions

Whereas the fastest runners are able to do well with just carbohydrate-containing fluids, slower runners will likely do better with not only fluids but also solids that provide more calories and also a flavor change. (Just how many hours in a row can you consume sports drinks and gels without getting "sugared-out"?) There is no magic to the special sports foods (e.g., gels, sports beans, energy bars) that are available at your local running store. These engineered foods are simply pre-wrapped and convenient. Use them if you prefer, but also know you could save money by eating sugar cookies and twizzlers. Fanny packs or running shorts with multiple pockets are a good way to carry your snacks.

"My stomach doesn't tolerate the typical "race" foods and drinks like Gatorade and Gu. But I've learned I can easily substitute fruit juice, granola and other foods that are a part of my standard diet."

Jill Roberts, Tampa, FL

Commercial Sports Foods

As a new runner, you likely feel confused by the plethora of commercial sports foods from which to choose. A multitude of businesses have jumped on the bandwagon to create products that appeal to a variety of runners, from those with special dietary requests (gluten-free, vegan) to those who are just plain hungry and want a "politically correct" candy bar (Marathon Bar).

When it comes to what to buy, there is no "best choice"; you simply need to experiment to determine what products satisfy your taste buds and settle well. Most of the sports products claim to be easy to digest, but you will have to determine that for yourself. Just keep in mind "real food" (dried figs, gummy bears, chocolate milk) can often do the same job at a lower price. Commercial sports foods tend to be more about convenience than necessity; they can make fueling easier for busy runners.

Below is a comprehensive (but unlikely complete) list of various types of assorted sports fuels and foods. Perhaps it will help you untangle the jungle of choices. Don't be swayed by a product's name; it might be more powerful than the sports food itself...

SPORTS DRINKS
With sodium (and perhaps other electrolytes):
Gatorade, Edge Energy, Hydro-Boom!, GU2O, CytoMax, Clif Shot Electrolyte, Motor Tabs

All natural without dye/food coloring:
First Endurance EFS, Clif Shot Electrolyte Drink, Hammer Nutrition HEED, Recharge

Extra sodium (Good idea if you plan to exercise for more than 2 hours in the heat):
Gatorade Endurance, PowerBar Endurance, E-Fuel, First Endurance EFS, Clif Shot Electrolyte Drink, E-Load, Hydro Pro Cooler

Added "buffers": Cytomax, Perpetuem, Revenge Sport

Extra carbs: Perpetuem, Carbo-Pro

Added protein (May reduce post-exercise muscle soreness);
Amino Vital, Perpetuem, Accelerade, Revenge Pro

Sports drinks for dieters (i.e., lower calorie):
PowerAde Option, Gatorade G2, Ultima Replenisher, Xtra LowOz, Propel, Nuun

GELS

(Test with these during training. They can taste very sweet and are common contributors to diarrhea)
Gu, Carb-BOOM!, Clif Shot, Honey Stinger (all natural)

Extra sodium: PowerBar Gel, Crank Sports e-Gel

Added protein: Accel Gel, Endless Edge, Hammer Gel

Added caffeine: GU Espresso Love, Clif Shot Mocha, Cola and Strawberry; Carb-BOOM Chocolate Cherry, Hammer Gel Espresso, PowerBar Gel Double Latte, Tangerine, Chocolate, Green Apple and Strawberry-banana; Honey Stinger Ginsting and Strawberry

Added extras: EAS Energy Gel (taurine)

ENDURANCE FOOD

Jelly Belly Sports Beans (a jelly bean with sodium). Clif Shot Bloks (a soft gummi candy in a block), Sharkies (organic fruit chew), SPIZ ("liquid food")

RECOVERY DRINKS (Carbs with a little protein)

Amino Vital, First Endurance E3, EAS Endurathon, Perpetuem, PowerBar Recovery Drinks, Recoverite, Go Energy Drink, Endurox R4, Gatorade Nutrition Shake, Hormel's Great Shake, GNC's Distance, Clif Shot Recovery Drink, First Endurance Ultragen

ENERGY DRINKS: (Concentrated sugar, often with added caffeine):

Red Bull, Rock Star, Monster, Rebound-fx, Full Throttle

ENERGY BARS (should be eaten for extra energy, not as a meal replacement):
All natural/organic (have no added vitamins or minerals):
Clif Bar, Peak Energy, Perfect 10, Clif Nectar, Clif Mojo, Lara Bar, Optimum, TrailMix HoneyBar, Odwalla Bar, PowerBar Nut Naturals, Honey Stinger Bars, Kashi Bars

Granola-type bars: PowerBar Harvest, Nature Valley Granola Bar, Quaker Chewy Bars, Nutri-Grain Bar, Fig Newtons

WOMEN'S BARS (fewer calories; soy, calcium, iron and folic acid):
PowerBar Pria, Amino Vital Fit, Luna Bar, Balance Oasis

40-30-30 Bars:	Balance Bar, ZonePerfect
Kosher:	Pure Fit, Lara Bar, Extend Bar, Raw Revolution
Dairy-free:	Clif Nectar, Pure Fit, Perfect 10, Lara Bar, Clif Builder's Bar
Gluten-free:	Perfect 10, Elev8Me, Hammer Bar, Clif Nectar, EnvirKids Rice Cereal Bar; Omega Smart Bars, Odwalla Bar, Clif Builder's Bar, Extend Bar, Zing Bar
Fructose-free:	JayBar
Vegan:	Pure Fit, Lara Bar, Hammer Bar, Vega Whole Food Raw Energy Bar, Clif Builder's Bar, Perfect 10, Raw Revolution
Low fiber:	Balance Bar
Bars with caffeine:	Peak Energy Plus
Vitamin & protein-pumped candy bar:	Marathon Bar; Detour Bar
Recovery bar (4:1 carb:pro ratio):	PowerBar Performance

Undesired Pit Stops

Many runners fear that fluids or foods taken during exercise will cause diarrhea. Diarrhea commonly occurs in novice runners, whose intestinal tracts are not fully adjusted to the jostling that happens while running. With experience, the problem tends to abate, but some experienced runners carry toilet paper with them.

If you fear diarrhea attacks, experiment during training with dietary changes to see if less fiber (such as bran cereals and lots of whole grains, fruits and vegetables) can reduce the problem. Or try less milk (switch to lactose-free milk products). Some runners simply need to abstain from food for three or four hours pre-event.

Diarrhea is also common among runners who become dehydrated and sweat off more than 4 percent of their body weight (6 pounds for a 150-pound person; 3 kg/70 kg). Hence, the fluids you drink may actually help prevent diarrhea, not cause it. I once talked to a runner who tried to abstain from drinking anything—even water—during a marathon in fear it would upset his stomach. He held off as long as he could without fluids. Then when he did succumb, he got diarrhea. Although he blamed the diarrhea on the drink, I tend to think the lack of prior fluid intake was the bigger problem.

Summary
Preventing dehydration and low blood sugar is crucial to being able to not only survive but also enjoy a run that lasts longer than 60 to 90 minutes. The fluids and foods that you consume during your long runs should be an extension of your carbohydrate-rich daily training diet. Because each runner has individual tolerances and preferences, you want to learn by trial and error during training what foods and fluids settle best and contribute to top competitive performance.

Thinking About Running a Marathon?

As a new runner who is enjoying the process of getting fit and being able to run further and further, you might have your eye on a marathon sometime in your future. Perhaps you are curious about that pre-marathon ritual and reward called "carbo-loading." "Carbo-loading" means more than just stuffing yourself with pasta, so here are some tips for future reference.

Pre-marathon Training Diet

Eat a carbohydrate-rich sports diet every day as the foundation for every meal to develop a tried-and-true training diet that will support 26.2 miles of marathoning.
- On your long training runs, practice eating your planned pre-marathon breakfast.
- Start some of your long training runs at the time you'll be starting the marathon.
- Learn how much pre-exercise food you can eat and then still exercise comfortably.
- Practice drinking the sports drink that will be available on race day as well as any mid-run foods (gels, fruit) you plan to eat.

The Week Before the Marathon:

- Taper off your training so that your muscles have the opportunity to become fully fueled.
- Keep your eating about the same. The 600 to 1,000 calories you generally expend during training will be used to fuel your muscles.
- Be sure that you are carbo-loading, not fat-loading. That is, instead of having one roll with butter for 200 calories, have two plain rolls for 200 calories. Enjoy pasta with tomato sauce rather than oily or cheesey toppings.
- Continue to eat a small serving of low-fat proteins as the accompaniment to the meal (not the main focus).

The Day Before the Marathon

- Expect to gain about three to four pounds of water weight. For every ounce of carbohydrate stored in your body, you store about three ounces of water.
- Instead of relying upon a huge pasta dinner the night before the marathon, you might want to enjoy a substantial carbo-feast at breakfast or lunch. This earlier meal allows plenty of time for the food to move through your system. Or, eat at both times!
- Drink extra water, juices, and even carbohydrate-rich soft drinks, if desired. Abstain from too much wine, beer and alcoholic beverages.

Marathon Morning
- Eat a tried-and-true breakfast that will settle well.
- Drink plenty of fluids. Take your preferred beverage with you so you'll have it available at the race.
- If you are coffee drinker, enjoy your standard morning brew.

During the Marathon
- Prevent dehydration by drinking on a schedule.
- Maintain a normal blood sugar level, by consuming about 200 to 300 calories of carbs during the event.

Note: These topics are discussed in detail in Chapters 9, 10 and 11.

Two Sample High Carbohydrate Menus

Menu #1		Menu #2	
Breakfast	Wheaties	Breakfast	Oatmeal
	Milk, 1% lowfat		Milk
	Bagel		Raisins
	Honey		Brown sugar
	Orange juice		Apple juice
Lunch	Whole grain bread, 2 slices	Lunch	Baguette
	Peanut butter		Lean meat
	Jelly		Lettuce, tomato
	Fruit yogurt		Fruit yogurt
	Pretzels		Grape juice
Pre-run snack	Apple	Pre-run snack	Fig Newtons
	Graham crackers		Low fat milk
Dinner	Chicken breast	Dinner	Spaghetti
	Rice		Tomato sauce with a little meat
	Broccoli		Italian bread
	Dinner roll		Salad with light dressing
	Sherbert		(Canned) peaches

Oatmeal Raisin Cookies

These cookies digest easily and can be used for energy during a long run, or enjoyed with a glass of skim milk (or a latte) before or after a run. Because they are made with (healthful) canola oil, they are soft and cakey.

The recipe makes about 5 dozen cookies—enough to feed a whole team of runners. If you are cooking for yourself, you might want to cut the recipe in half!

1 1/4 cup	(300 ml)	milk
1 cup	(240 ml)	canola oil
2 eggs or 4 egg whites		
2 teaspoons	(10 ml)	vanilla
3/4 cup	(150 g)	white sugar
1 cup	(180 g)	packed brown sugar
4 cups	(360 g)	uncooked oatmeal
2 teaspoons	(10 g)	baking soda
2 teaspoons	(10 g)	salt
2 teaspoons	(10 g)	cinnamon
3 cups	(360 g)	flour, half whole-wheat, half white, as desired
1 cup	(150 g)	raisins

1. Preheat the oven to 350°F (175°C).
2. In a large bowl, mix together the milk, oil, sugar, oatmeal, eggs and vanilla. Beat well.
3. Add the soda, salt and cinnamon; mix well, then gently stir in the flour, then the raisins.
4. Drop by rounded tablespoons onto an ungreased baking sheet.
5. Bake for 15 to 18 minutes or until firm when lightly tapped with a finger.

Yield:	5 dozen cookies
Nutrition Information:	
Total calories:	6,500
Calories per cookie:	110
Carbohydrate	16 g
Protein	2 g
Fat	4 g

Reprinted with permission from Nancy Clark's Sports Nutrition Guidebook, Fourth Edition (Human Kinetics, 2008)

Chapter 12
Recovery: What to Eat After You Run

As a novice runner, you are unlikely to be doing exhaustive workouts that require rapid refueling. If you progress to double workouts or Ironman triathlon training, the recovery diet will become more and more important. During this process of transforming from a novice jogger to a competitive runner, you do need to put some thought into your recovery plan so you get into the habit of refueling your muscles.

All too often, I talk with runners who hesitate to refuel, thinking "That run killed my appetite, so this is a good time to NOT eat. I want to lose body fat, so why would I want to replace what I just burned off—when I am not even hungry?"

Here are four reasons why:
1. You'll feel more energetic the rest of the day, if you refuel properly.
2. Rapid refueling tends to reduce post-exercise muscle soreness.
3. Your muscles will be able to better repair little injuries that occurred during the run and your body will be better able to endure repeated days (and hopefully months and years) of workouts that might get progressively longer and harder.
4. When your appetite does return (as happens when your body temperature returns to normal), you will likely feel ravenous, and might easily succumb to overeating. To lose weight, you want to create a calorie deficit at the end of the day, not live with hunger during the day. (See Chapter 14 on weight management.)

The bottom line: before you dash off to a post-workout obligation (school, work, meeting, etc.), be sure to eat a little bit of something.

"When I first started to run, I used to crash really hard after long runs. Now I have learned the value of chocolate milk for a good recovery drink that replenishes my system."

John McGrath, Newton, MA

Recovery Options

What should you eat to optimize recovery? I recommend a post-exercise snack that includes a foundation of carbs to refuel the depleted glycogen stores and a little protein to repair the muscle damage. You don't need to eat tons of food—about 100 to 400 calories, or enough to carry you to your next meal. Most runners tend to naturally follow this pattern with repeated snacks and meals, assuming they are not "dieting" or "too busy" to eat.

Good carb + protein recovery choices include:
- fruit yogurt
- chocolate milk
- cereal with milk
- turkey on a baguette
- chicken dinner with rice and vegetables
- spaghetti with meat sauce

If you are refueling on the run, carry with you:
- trail mix (nuts and raisins)
- bagel with peanut butter
- Go-gurt (liquid yogurt)
- Energy bar with 3 to 4 times as many carbs as protein

Some marathoners like commercial recovery drinks, like Accelerade or Endurox. Just remember: these engineered foods lack all the health-protective nutrients that you get in "real food," so be sure to balance them into an overall healthful diet.

Sometimes new runners overextend themselves and feel nauseous after a run. In such a case, try to drink a little ginger ale, chicken broth or chicken noodle soup, or nibble on a few saltines or pretzels. The sooner you can get fluids, carbs and sodium into your system, the better you will start to feel.

"I have found that I recover much more quickly if I sip on orange juice and eat at least half a banana."

Shelley Smith, Highlands Ranch, CO

How much should you drink? As a new runner, you are unlikely to be exercising so long that you become dehydrated, but you should replace fluid losses as soon as possible to help your body restore normal water balance. You'll know that you are well hydrated when you need to urinate every 2 to 4 hours and have pale-colored urine. Refer to Chapter 9 for a urine color chart and more information on hydration tactics.

As to what to drink, water generally does the job of replacing sweat losses for new runners, and recovery snacks can offer the needed carbs, protein and sodium. Remember, you have unlikely depleted yourself, so you need not fret about making the best recovery choice. I just want you to get into the habit of taking proper care of your body.

Popular Recovery Foods

Your muscles are most receptive to replacing depleted glycogen stores immediately after exercise. By feeding them carbohydrates, preferably with a little bit of protein, you can optimize the recovery process. Don't get hung-up on the recommended 4 to 1 ratio of carbs to protein; just enjoy wholesome carb-based foods that will refuel depleted glycogen stores. Include a little protein to repair and build muscles, but do not emphasize the protein.

For long distance runners, a good target is 60 to 90 grams of carbs every two hours or so.

Some popular choices include:

Fluids (8 oz; 240 ml):	Carb (g)	Protein (g)
Gatorade	14	--
Coke	26	--
Cranberry Juice	43	--
Accelerade	14	3
Chocolate milk	26	8
Yogurt, flavored	40	10

Solids:		
Trail mix (raisins, granola, nuts)	40	10
PowerBar, chocolate	45	10
Cheerios w/ milk	50	12
Pasta, 2 cups + meat sauce	100	20

Do you need extra salt to replace what you lose in sweat?
As a novice runner, you are unlikely to be losing gallons of sweat, nor significant amounts of sodium. During three hours of sweaty exercise, you might lose about 1,800 to 5,600 milligrams of sodium. Since the average 150-pound person's body contains about 97,000 milligrams of sodium, this 2 to 6 percent loss is relatively insignificant. If you find yourself craving salt, then you should respond appropriately by eating salty foods such as salted pretzels, soups, crackers and/or baked potatoes or other foods sprinkled with salt.

Do you need extra protein?
While eating a little protein along with recovery carbohydrates is a smart choice, you should not "protein load" and eat a protein-based recovery diet. That is, do not choose a protein bar or protein shake for your recovery food. Instead have a carb shake (i.e., a fruit smoothie made with yogurt and fruit) that offers a foundation of carbs and a little bit of protein.

What about beer…?
If you choose to reward yourself with a beer, be sure to first drink some water and eat something (anything!) so that you are not drinking alcohol on an empty stomach. For each beer, have a non-alcoholic drink (water, soft drink) to moderate alcohol's dehydrating effect.

Remember to take rest days
Rest is an essential part of your training program. If you feel compelled to run to "burn off calories," keep reading. The section on Weight Management (Chapters 14 and 15) might help you accept rest days as an important part of even a weight reduction program.

Sunshine Refresher

Light and refreshing, this is a welcomed recovery drink after a hot workout. It offers carbs to refuel muscles, protein to build and heal muscles, and fluid to replace sweat losses. But more importantly, it tastes great!

8 ounces	(230 g)	plain or vanilla yogurt
1/2 cup	(120 ml)	skim or lowfat milk
1/2 cup	(120 ml)	orange juice
8 ice cubes		
1 tablespoon	(15 ml)	honey, sugar or sweetener as desired

1. Combine all ingredients in a blender.

2. Whip until smooth and frothy.

3. Enjoy!

Yield:	1 large serving (for a thirsty runner!)
Nutrition Information:	
Total calories:	250 (made with skim milk and yogurt)
Carbohydrate:	50 g
Protein:	6 g
Fat:	—

SECTION IV

Chapter 13
Creating a Calorie Budget

Many runners are on the "see food diet"; they see food and they eat it. They eat when they are hungry and stop when they are content. They naturally regulate a proper calorie intake.

WEIGHT AND RUNNERS —THE RIGHT DIET

Other runners see food and try to not eat it because they want to lose weight. They deem food as "fattening" and counter to their desires to be leaner, lighter runners. They often undereat by day and then overeat later in the evening.

As an up-and-coming athlete, you want to eat your calories evenly throughout the day. If you want to lose weight, you can do that at night, when you are sleeping! (See Chapter 14.) You need to eat *enough* at breakfast and lunch to support both an active life and your training program. Eating (wholesome) calories evenly throughout the day invests in high energy, added stamina, strength and smooth running, to say nothing of better health.

If you struggle with energy lags late morning or mid-afternoon, you might want to assess how many calories you are eating at breakfast and lunch, and then compare that to how many calories your body requires. Just like it's helpful to know how much money you can spend when you go shopping, knowing your calorie budget can help you determine how much you can eat to:

• lose desired weight and maintain energy for running.
• fuel-up and refuel from workouts.
• train better.
• feel good about your eating.

A calorie-counting approach to eating can be particularly helpful to runners who feel tired all the time. It can help you understand why you are tired. For example, if you skip breakfast and lunch (i.e., eat 0 calories), you can clearly see why you lack energy for your afternoon training session. If you are weight-conscious, calorie information allows you to determine how much food you can eat for fuel yet still lose body fat. Once you get in touch with how you feel when you eat appropriately, you'll be able to naturally regulate your food intake—without counting calories.

"Knowing my calorie budget has been incredibly helpful. Now I know how much is OK to eat. I no longer feel guilty if I have two granola bars AND a yogurt for breakfast!"

Dave Westin, Brockton, MA

Calculating Your Calorie Needs

Here's an easy formula to help you estimate your calorie needs. For more personalized advice, I highly recommend you consult with a registered dietitian (RD) who specializes in sports nutrition. Visit the American Dietetic Association's referral network at www.eatright.org or www.SCANdpg.org to find a local sports dietitian.

1. To estimate your resting metabolic rate (RMR), that is, the amount of calories you need to simply breathe, pump blood and be alive:

    Multiply your weight (or a good weight for your body) by 10 calories per pound (or 22 calories per kilogram).

    _____weight (lbs) x 10 calories/lb = _____ calories for your RMR

Example: If you weigh 120 pounds, you need approximately 1,200 calories (120 x 10) to simply do nothing all day except exist. If you are significantly overweight, use an adjusted weight: the weight that is halfway between your desired weight and your current weight.

2. Add more calories for daily activity—apart from your running and other purposeful exercise.

    *   50% x RMR if you are moderately active throughout the day

    *   approx. 30-40% if you are sedentary

    *   approx. 60-70% if you are very active (apart from your running or walking)

    50% x _____RMR = _____ calories for daily activity

Example: a moderately active 120-pound woman who requires 1,200 calories for her resting metabolic rate needs about 600 more calories for activities of daily living. This totals 1,800 calories per day—without running.

3. Add more calories for your purposeful exercise. The general rule of thumb is 100 calories per mile, but more precisely, this depends upon your weight.

Body Weight lbs (kg)	Calories per Mile
120 (55)	95
140 (64)	110
160 (73)	125
180 (82)	140

_____exercise calories + _____daily activity + _____RMR = _____total calories

Example: a 120-pound woman who runs five miles per day burns about 475 calories while running. For simplicity, let's just say 500 calories. This brings her to about 2,300 calories per day to maintain her weight (500 running + 600 moderate daily activity + 1,200 RMR = 2,275 or more simply, 2,300).

Note: After a hard workout, runners tend to rest, recover and burn fewer calories than usual during the rest of their day. Observe if this happens with you. That is, do you tend to sit more than usual—reading more or watching more TV—after having done a tiring run? If so, adjust your calorie needs accordingly!

4. To lose weight, target 80 percent of total calorie needs.
   80% x _____total calories = _____ calories to reduce weight

Example: .80 x 2,300 calories = 1,840 calories, or more simply 1,800 calories/day

(Refer to Chapter 14 for more guidance on weight loss.)

5. Now, take your calorie budget and divide it into three or four parts of the day. For the 120-pound woman on a diet, this comes to:

	Calories			Calories
Breakfast/snack	600	OR	Breakfast	500
Lunch/snack	600		Lunch	500
Dinner/snack	600		Lunch #2	300
			Dinner	500

The next step is to read food labels and get calorie information from websites such as www.fitday.com or www.calorieking.com to become familiar with the calorie content of the foods you commonly eat. Now, fuel your body according to the rules for a well-balanced diet.

Calorie Need of Runners

Here are approximate calorie needs for runners of different weights who remain moderately active throughout the day.

Take note: After a 10-miler, you may be ready to take a nice long nap, and that would reduce your overall calorie needs for the day! Be sure to adjust your calories according to your 24-hour energy expenditure...

Weight	Approximate calorie needs for:		
lbs (kg)	no running	with 5 mile-run	with 10-mile run
120 (55)	1,800	2,300	2,700
140 (64)	2,100	2,650	3,200
160 (73)	2,400	3,000	3,650
180 (82)	2,700	3,400	4,100

Hungry All the Time?

I commonly hear runners complain, "Ever since I started training longer distances, I've been hungry all the time." They often feel confused by hunger and sometimes even feel guilty they are always eager to eat.

Hunger is normal; it is simply your body's way of talking to you, requesting fuel. After all, the more you exercise, the hungrier you will get and the more fuel you need. Plan to fuel up or refuel at least every four hours. You should not spend your day feeling hungry—even if you are on a reducing diet. (See Chapter 14). If your 8:00 A.M. breakfast finds you hungry earlier than noon, your breakfast simply contained too few calories. You need a supplemental midmorning snack or a bigger breakfast that supplies about 25 to 35 % of your day's calories.

Come noontime, instead of thinking something is wrong with you because you are hungry again, enjoy lunch as being the second-most-important meal of the day. Morning runners, in particular, need a hearty lunch to refuel their muscles; afternoon runners need a respectable lunch and afternoon snack/second lunch to fuel for their after-work training.

Whereas some runners like to satisfy their appetites with big meals, others prefer to divide their calories into mini-meals eaten every two hours. Eat however suits your training schedule and lifestyle. But whatever you do, eat when you are physically hungry. Hunger is simply your body's request for fuel. (The next chapter offers strategies for managing overeating, that is misusing food as a "drug" to calm and reward yourself; keep reading!)

Pasta with Spinach and Cottage Cheese

Runners like food that is simple, performance-enhancing and delicious. This recipe meets those standards! Plus, it's made with ingredients that can be kept on hand and don't spoil quickly. For fastest preparation, use quick-cooking angel hair pasta.

6 ounces	(170 g)	pasta, such as angel hair
1 10-ounce	(280 g)	box frozen chopped spinach
1 cup	(230 g)	cottage cheese, preferably low fat
$^1/_4$ cup	(22 g)	grated Parmesan cheese
Salt and pepper, as desired		

Optional: Dash of cayenne, sprinkling of garlic powder, oregano, basil.

1. Cook the pasta according to the directions on the box.

2. While the pasta is cooking, thaw and cook the spinach in the microwave oven or on the stovetop.

3. Drain the cooked spinach; add the cottage cheese, Parmesan and seasonings as desired. Mix well and then add the cooked pasta.

Yield:	2 servings
Nutrition Information:	
Total calories:	950
Calories per serving:	475
Carbohydrate:	71 g
Protein:	36 g
Fat:	5 g

Winning Recipe

Chapter 14
Weight Reduction for New Runners

Many people start running with the goals of improving their health and losing undesired body fat. Without question, you will improve your health and fitness. But you cannot assume your body fat will simply melt away. As coach Lloyd Burnett of Mission, TX said, "I once trained three new marathoners who each lost 20 pounds in less than 6 months. Each of them made the commitment to be conscious about their calories and overall food intake. My training partner and I, on the other hand, have run almost 20 marathons but we each still weigh 220 pounds. I love my beer and he loves his tortillas. We're not willing to commit to the diet part of the event, even though we see the results all around us."

"I have been doing marathons for two years. Like the majority of runners, I was hoping to lose weight, but that has not been the case for me. Some of my training buddies have even gained weight. Exercise alone does not suffice!"

Becky Goodrum, Cleveland, OH

How to Lose Weight and Have Energy to Run

I spend hours helping runners who are fighting the battle of the bulge. Inevitably, the first words they say to me are, "I know what I *should* do to lose weight. I just don't do it." They think they should follow a strict diet with rigid rules and regulations. Wrong. Diets don't work. If diets did work, every dieter would be as thin as desired.

The key to losing weight is to:
- stop thinking about *going on a diet*.
- start learning *how to eat healthfully*.

If you are dieting by day, only to overeat at night, think again.

How Much Is OK to Eat?

As I outlined in Chapter 13, most runners can lose weight on 1,800 to 2,200 calories (or more), This is far from a starvation diet! To determine just how much you can appropriately eat, refer back to Chapter 13. Note that your body requires a significant amount of energy to simply exist: pump blood, breathe, produce urine, grow hair and maintain your bodily functions. Running boosts your calorie needs a little bit, but not as much as you may expect.

To lose weight, you want to cut back on your food intake by just a little bit (for example, drink less soda, use less butter) while you add on exercise. Don't get over-zealous and cut your food intake in half, with hopes of losing weight quickly. That's a big mistake. Runners who try to lose weight quickly tend to get too hungry, "blow the diet", and end up gaining weight quickly—not what they wanted!

Food records can be extremely useful to help you understand why you have gained weight in the first place and what you need to do to lose it. For example, by recording *everything* you eat, you might notice that you:

- eat when reading and don't even notice the portion.

- eat too little at breakfast and lunch, only to overindulge at night.

- diet Monday through Thursday, then splurge on weekends.

If you are willing to keep accurate food records, you will probably be more successful with your weight reduction program. That's because people who keep food records tend to eat about 20 percent fewer calories—and that is a sustainable reducing diet.

"I frequently see people gain weight when they start running. They believe running gives them license to eat anything and everything. Unfortunately, a 3,000-calorie dessert still shows up on the butt."

John Correia, San Diego, CA

Five Keys to Successful Weight Reduction

Using your calorie guidelines, you can lose weight with the following five keys to successful weight reduction.

Key #1. Eat just a little bit less. Don't get too hungry or you'll blow your diet. As I said before, if you are trying to lose weight by eating as little as possible and exercising as hard as you can, think again. The less you eat, the more likely you are to blow your diet. Even if you can successfully restrict your intake, the less you eat, the more your body adjusts to having fewer calories. You will start to conserve energy—similar to what a bear does in winter when food is scarce. That is, your metabolic rate will drop and you'll feel lethargic, cold, moody and lack energy to run.

As I mentioned above, most of my clients who are new runners follow 1,800-to 2,000-calorie reducing diets. This is far more than their self-imposed 800-to 1,200-calorie starvation diets that ended in food binges. By simply knocking off fried foods (fried chicken, chips, French fries), sugary drinks and fatty foods (butter, mayonnaise, excess salad dressing), you can create a small but effective calorie deficit. You will still be able to eat enough carbs to fuel your muscles, and you will have enough energy to enjoy your training. At the end of dinner, you want to feel "not quite full"; this is much different than feeling hungry. When you wake up in the morning, you should feel ready to eat breakfast.

"I started dieting at the same time I started running longer distances. I'd 'hit the wall' much too early and I quickly learned: Don't try to lose weight while training for long distances. Dieting depletes running fuel reserves needed for longer runs."

Jim Lentz, Naperville, IL

Key #2. Be sure that you eat more during the day, so that you'll be able to eat less (diet) at night. For an appropriate reducing program, I recommend that you divide your calories evenly throughout the day. Your goal is to eat on a schedule that prevents hunger. Because people (especially runners) tend to get hungry at least every four hours, an appropriate eating pattern for a 1,800 to 2,200-calorie *reduction* diet might look like this:

Meal	Time	Calories
Breakfast:	8 A.M.	500 to 600
Lunch:	Noon	500 to 600
Lunch #2/Snack:	4 P.M.	400
Run:	6 P.M.	
Dinner:	8 P.M.	400 to 600

For most new runners, this means you'll eat more than you might be currently eating at breakfast, lunch and afternoon snack/second lunch, but less at dinner (and little or nothing after dinner). You should eat enough to feel content after the first three meals, and not quite full after dinner.

Your training program may require creative meal scheduling if you exercise during meal times. For example, if you exercise at 6 P.M.—potentially at the height of your hunger—you might enjoy your run more if you eat part of your dinner before you run. For example, trade in your 100-calorie dinner potato for a 100-calorie banana at 5:00 P.M. Similarly, if you exercise at 6:00 A.M., you might enjoy greater energy if you eat part of your breakfast beforehand, such as a slice of toast and a glass of juice, and then eat a yogurt with granola afterwards to recover from the workout and satisfy your hunger. (As I mentioned in Chapter 10, you need to experiment with pre-exercise food to determine the right amount of calories that boost your energy without making you feel heavy and sluggish.)

Some runners believe that exercising "on empty"—for example, running first thing in the morning before breakfast—helps them to burn more fat. While this may be true, keep in mind that *burning* fat does not equate to *losing* body fat. To lose body fat, you need to create a calorie *deficit* for the whole day (not just during workouts). If you exercise on empty, you'll lack the fuel you need to run longer or stronger. Hence, you'll burn fewer calories than if you had fueled your body properly before you started to run. You may also experience extreme hunger later in the day and end up raiding the cookie jar.

Key #3. Eat an appropriate amount of fat. If you are currently eating a high-fat diet filled with butter, mayonnaise, salad dressing, French fries and pepperoni, you should cut back on these and other fatty foods. Excess dietary fat easily turns into excess body fat, if not clogged arteries.

On the other hand, if you are trying to knock *all* the fat out of your diet—thinking that if you eat fat, you'll instantly gain body fat—think again and see Chapter 8. Fat can be helpful for dieters because it takes longer to digest and provides a nice feeling of satisfaction that can prevent you from scrounging around the kitchen, looking for something tasty to eat. Runners who try to eat a very low fat diet commonly live with a nagging hunger, to say nothing of feelings of denial and deprivation.

One study reported that dieters who were instructed to eat 1,200 calories of a high-fat diet actually lost more body fat than the group who were instructed to eat 1,200 calories of a very-low-fat diet. Why? Because the high-fat dieters were better able to comply with their regimen. You, too, may enjoy better success with weight loss if you give yourself a reasonable calorie and fat budget to spend on the foods that you truly enjoy eating. (Refer to Chapter 8 for more information on what a 25-percent fat diet looks like.) There is a diet portion of any food—including French fries and cookies!

Key #4. Try to lose weight when life is calm. Stressful times are often poor times to try to reduce body fat. When life is stressful, you may need to let go of your goal to lose fat and focus instead on not *gaining* weight. Remember: You don't have to lose weight every day; some days can be maintain days.

In the scheme of life, fitness is more important than fatness (in terms of health, that is). So during stressful times, focus on fitness, and on exercising regularly to help manage your stress. Make the effort to eat every four hours to keep your appetite under control. If you are both stressed and hungry, you can too easily succumb to overeating (even though no amount of food will solve any problem).

Key #5. Have realistic weight goals. Weight is more than a matter of willpower; genetics plays a large role. If you are exercising regularly, fueling appropriately during the day, eating lighter at night, and waking up hankering for breakfast—but still have not lost weight, perhaps you have an unrealistic weight goal? Perhaps you have no excess fat to lose and are already lean for your genetic blueprint?

Like it or not, weight is more than a matter of willpower. Although you might wish for a sleeker physique, nature might want you to be softer. You can remodel your body to a certain extent, but you cannot totally redesign it. Plain and simple, runners, like dogs, come in varying sizes and shapes. No one body type is right or wrong.

In order to determine an appropriate weight for your body, I recommend you stop looking at the scale and start looking at your family tree. Imagine yourself at a family reunion.

- How do you compare to other members of your family?
- Are you currently leaner than they are? Fatter? The same?
- If you are leaner, are you struggling to maintain that low weight?
- If you are significantly leaner, you may already be underfat for your body.

"Do not be obsessed with the numbers on the scale. With time and training, you will learn at what weight you can perform well. Listening to your body is more accurate than any scale."

Mike Czech, Edison, NJ

Why Are You Eating?

Food has many roles. It satisfies hunger, fuels muscles, is a pleasurable part of social gatherings and celebrations, rewards us at the end of a stressful day, and has a calming effect. If you tend to eat for reasons other than hunger, think HALT and ask yourself, why am I eating? Am I—:

Hungry?

Angry or Anxious?

Lonely?

Tired?

If you are eating for reasons other than hunger, remember that no amount of food will solve any problem. Try not to start eating if you think you'll have problems stopping.

I counsel many runners who struggle to lose the final few pounds. Some of these runners are simply trying to get to a weight that is abnormal for their genetics. For example, many female runners despise their "fat thighs." They fail to understand that fat in the thigh area is sex-specific. It is a storehouse of fuel for potential pregnancy and breast-feeding and is *supposed* to be there. Just as women have breast tissue, women also have thigh tissue. Women have fatter thighs than men because women are *women*.

If you are wasting your time and energy complaining about your body, take a deep breath and relax. Life is a gift, too short to be spent obsessing about food and weight. Be appreciative of all your body can do for you—such as run—and stop criticizing your body for what it is not.

You can be fit, healthy, and happy at any size. You can also be miserable at your "perfect weight" if the cost of attaining that weight is yo-yo dieting, poor nutrition, lack of energy to exercise, guilt for eating, and a sense of failure that crushes your self-esteem. No weight will even be good enough to create happiness. Eat well, run well, and be well.

Summary

Food is fuel. You need to fuel your muscles appropriately even if you are trying to lose weight. Be realistic about your expectations and remember the thinnest runner may not be the fastest runner. Also remember the following keys to successful weight control:

1. Cut back only 100 to 300 calories a day; don't starve yourself.

2. Fuel during the day, then diet at night. If you wake up ready for breakfast, you have likely lost body fat overnight, while you were sleeping.

3. Include a little bit of (healthful) dietary fat at each meal to keep you from feeling hungry and also from feeling denied of tasty foods.

4. Strive to maintain weight on stress-filled days and lose weight on calmer days.

5. Honor your genetics and be realistic with your weight goals.

6. Win with good nutrition!

Target Weights

Although only nature knows the best weight for your body, the following guidelines offer a very general method to estimate a healthy weight range. Add or subtract 10 percent, according to your body frame and musculature. (Note: These guidelines do not work for very muscular runners.)

Women: 100 pounds (45 kg) for the first 5 feet (1.52 m) of height;
5 pounds (2.3 kg) per inch (2.5 cm) thereafter

Example: A woman who is 5' 6" could appropriately weigh 130 lbs, or 117 lbs at the lower end if she is petite or 143 lbs if she is muscular. (1.7 m; 59 kg, 53-65 kg)

Men: 106 pounds (48 kg) for the first 5 feet (1.52 m) of height;
6 pounds (2.7 kg) per inch (2.5 cm) thereafter

Example: A man who is 5' 10" could appropriately weigh 166 lbs, or 150 lbs at the lower end if he is petite or 182 lbs if he is muscular. (1.8 m; 75.5 kg, 68-83 kg)

Although runners commonly want to be lighter than the average person, heed this message: If you are striving to weigh significantly less than the weight estimated by this general guideline, think again. Pay attention to the genetic design for your body and don't struggle to get too light. The best weight goal is to be fit and healthy rather than sleek and skinny. Even overweight runners can be fit and healthy!

For more information:
http://www.cdc.gov/nccdphp/dnpa/healthyweight/

This website, sponsored by the Center for Disease Control, offers abundant information on how to lose weight by eating well. You'll find information on calories, meal planning, exercise and weight reduction tips for the long run.

Frozen Fruit Nuggets

Every major medical association reminds us to eat more fruit. Here's an easy way to do that:

When you are confronted with well-ripened fruit that needs to get eaten before it spoils, freeze it as nuggets. Bananas are particularly good when frozen; they taste like banana ice cream! Plus, freezing them solves the "what-do-I-do-with-the-ripe-bananas" crisis.

After a hot run, pop a few frozen fruit nuggets into your mouth for a refreshing and welcome treat. Or, whip them up into a delightfully frosty shake with milk, juice or yogurt.

Your choice of:

- Grapes, removed from the stem
- Bananas, peeled and in chunks
- Strawberries, hulled
- Watermelon cubes
- Cantaloupe cubes
- Other fruits of your choice

1. Spread bite-size pieces of fruit on a flat pan and put it in the freezer for 1 hour.

2. When frozen, put the pieces into baggies, where they will be ready for you to eat when the munchies strike!

Nutrition Information

Serving size:	1 cup
Calories per serving:	approximately 50
Carbohydrate:	12 g
Protein:	trace
Fat:	trace

Winning Recipe

Chapter 15
Dieting Gone Awry

Too many new runners feel pressure to lose weight. They've been led to believe "thinner is better." Runners who strive to be "perfectly" thin commonly pay a high price: poor nutrition, poorly fueled muscles, stress fractures, nagging injuries, loss of menses (in women), to say nothing of reduced stamina, endurance and performance. For some, obsessions with food and weight culminate in disordered eating patterns, if not outright eating disorders. If you struggle with food, keep reading!

Runners and Weight

Weight tends to be a big issue among novice runners. Sometimes these runners are overfat and rightfully discontent with their undesired flab. Other times, they are actually lean and simply have distorted body images.

The Madison Avenue image that adorns every storefront and magazine ad leads us to believe that nature makes all people universally lean. Wrong! Nature makes us in different sizes and shapes, like it or not. If you are a woman, remember: Women need body fat to protect your ability to create and nourish healthy babies and to provide a storehouse of calories for pregnancy and breast-feeding. This essential body fat is stored not only in the breasts but also in the hips, abdomen and upper legs. Counter to Nature's plan, some women deem this fat as being undesirable.

Whereas 11 to 13 percent of a woman's body weight is essential fat stores, only 3 to 5 percent of a man's body weight is essential body fat. Hence, women who try to achieve the "cut look" of male runners commonly have to starve themselves—and end up obsessing about food as they struggle to reach an unnatural image.

If you are training harder and harder to lose body fat, stop! You should train to enhance performance, not to reshape your body. Exercise as punishment for having excess body fat is not sustainable, and commonly results in injuries. If all runners who are discontent with their weight could only learn to appreciate and love their bodies as being "good enough," eating disorders would be rare.

The Slow Metabolism Woes

Some runners perceive themselves as being energy-efficient and having to eat "less than they deserve." They express these complaints:

- "I eat less than my friends but I still don't lose weight. There must be something wrong with my metabolism."
- "I maintain weight on only 1,000 calories per day. I want to lose a few pounds, but I can't imagine eating any less."
- "I run at least eight miles every day and eat only one meal a day. I can't understand why I don't lose weight."

Does Nature slow an athlete's metabolism to protect him or her from getting too thin? Or, does the runner become very inactive when he or she is not exercising? That is, after a long run, runners can easily take a nap, read the paper or relax more than before they started training. (Prior to becoming runners, they might have mowed the lawn, played actively with their children and been more active throughout the entire day.) Hence, the trick to reversing "energy efficiency" may simply be to remain active throughout the entire day, not just when training.

Women, Running and Amenorrhea

If you are a woman who previously had regular menstrual periods but currently has stopped menstruating, you are experiencing amenorrhea. Although you may think the loss of menses is because you are too thin or are exercising too much, thinness and exercise are generally not the causes of amenorrhea. After all, many very thin athletes do have regular menses.

Why then, given a group of women who have a similar training program and the same low percent of body fat, do some experience menstrual problems and others don't? Runners with amenorrhea undereat to maintain their desired weight. The cost of achieving their desired leanness is inadequate calories and, consequently, loss of menses. Hence, athletic amenorrhea tends to be a nutritional problem and sometimes is a red flag for an eating disorder. If you stop having regular menstrual periods, be sure to consult with both your gynecologist and sports nutritionist for professional guidance.

"I'm saddened by how many women runners have eating disorders. I know, because I struggled with food for a while. I can pick out all the runners who are currently struggling. They think they have a secret but they don't.
I can remember how tired I used to be. Then, I started eating better and my running got better. I was surprised by how well food worked. It really helps runners to run better!"

Gordon Bakoulis, New York City, NY

Health Risks Associated with Amenorrhea

Although you may deem amenorrhea a desirable side effect of exercise because you no longer have to deal with the hassles and possible discomfort of monthly menstrual periods, amenorrhea can lead to undesirable problems that can interfere with your health and ability to perform at your best. These problems include:

- almost a three times higher incidence of stress fractures.

- premature osteoporosis (weakening of the bones) that can affect your bone health in the not-too-distant future.

- inability to conceive should you want to have a baby.

If the amenorrhea is caused by very restrictive eating, it can be a symptom of pain and unhappiness in your life. Note that the "absence of at least three consecutive menstrual cycles" is part of the American Psychiatric Association's definition for anorexia.

Amenorrheic women who resume menses can restore some of the bone density lost during their months of amenorrhea, particularly if they are younger than seventeen years. But they do not restore all of it. Your goal should be to minimize the damages of amenorrhea by eating appropriately and taking the proper steps to regain your menstrual periods. Remember: Food is fuel, healthful and health-giving, not a fattening enemy.

Resolving Amenorrhea

The possible changes required to resume menses include:

- training 5 to 15 percent less (50 minutes instead of an hour).

- consuming 10 percent more calories each week, until you ingest an appropriate amount given your activity level. For example, if you have been eating 1,000 calories a day, eat 100 more calories per day for a total of 1,100 total calories a day during the first week (or even for 2 to 3 days); eat a total of 1200 calories per day the second week; 1,300 the third week, and so on. (See Chapter 13 for how to determine an appropriate calorie intake.)

Some amenorrheic runners have resumed menses just with reduced exercise and no weight gain. Others resume menstruating after gaining less than five pounds (rather, rebuilding and restoring five pounds of health). And despite what you may think, this small amount of weight gain tends to include muscle-gain and does not result in your "getting fat."

How to Build a Better Food Plan

If you maintain weight despite eating minimal calories and are spending way too much time thinking about food, here's a sample food plan to help you start to fuel your body better. Gradually add 100 calories every 3 to 7 days (or every day, for that matter) and observe the benefits: you will likely feel stronger, happier, warmer; sleep better; have better workouts, and think less about food. Because you are adding essential (not excess) calories to get your body out of hibernation, you will be unlikely to "get fat."

Your best bet, to help you through this process of relearning how to eat appropriately, is to go to www.eatright.org or www.SCANdpg.org and use the referral networks to find a local sports dietitian who can provide personalized advice.

	Baseline Menu: 1,000 calories		How to increase by +100 calories/week X 8 weeks	Improved 1,800-calorie Menu	
Breakfast	Special K, 1 cup (30 g)	100	Week #5. Add 100 cals more cereal	Special K, 2 cups	200
			Week #1. Add banana: +100	Banana	100
	Milk, 1/2 cup	50		Milk 1/2 cup	50
	Apple, average	100		Apple	100
			Week #6: Add 14 almonds +100	Almonds, 14	100
Lunch	Salad	100		Salad	100
	Tuna, small can	100	Week #2. Larger can tuna: +100	Tuna, lg can	200
			Week #3 Add 1 cup yogurt: +100	Yogurt, 1 cup	100
			Week #7: Add crackers +100	Crackers	100
Snack	Energy bar	250		Energy bar	250
Dinner	Chicken breast, 4 oz	200		Chicken breast	200
	Broccoli, 2 cups	100		Broccoli, 2 cups	100
			Week #4. Add 1/2 cup rice +100 cals	Rice, 1/2 cup	100
			Week #8: Add 1 cup milk	Milk, 1 cup	100
	Total: 1,000 calories				**1,800**

Steps to Resolve Eating Disorders

If you are spending too much time obsessing about food, weight and exercise, seek help and information on these websites:

National Eating Disorders Association (information and referral network)
www.NationalEatingDisorders.org

American Dietetic Association (referral network)
www.eatright.org

Something Fishy Website on Eating Disorders (information and referral network)
www.something-fishy.org

Gurze Books (recommended self-help books)
www.bulimia.com

If you suspect your training partner or friend is struggling with food issues, speak up! Anorexia and bulimia are self-destructive eating behaviors that may signal underlying depression and can be life threatening. Here are some helpful tips:

- Approach the person gently but be persistent. Say that you are worried about her health. She, too, may be concerned about her loss of concentration, light-headedness, or chronic fatigue. These health changes are more likely to be a stepping-stone to accepting help, since the person clings to food and exercise for feelings of control and stability.
- Don't discuss weight or eating habits. Address the fundamental problems of life. Focus on unhappiness as the reason for seeking help. Point out what you see: ("I see you are very anxious. You look tired, are snappy and easily irritated lately." Emphasize she doesn't have to be that way.
- Give her a list of resources (above), and if you are really worried, make an appointment with a doctor, counselor, or sports dietitian and take her there yourself.

Remember that you are not responsible for resolving the eating issues and can only try to help. Your power comes from using community resources, eating disorders clinic and health professionals.

The following tips may help you resume menses or at least rule out nutrition-related factors.

1. *Throw away the bathroom scale.* Rather than striving to achieve a certain number on the scale, let your body weigh what it weighs. Focus on how healthy you feel and how well you perform, rather than on the number you weigh.

2. *If you have weight to lose, don't crash-diet but rather moderately cut back on your food intake by about 20 percent.* Rapid weight loss may predispose you to amenorrhea. By following a healthy reducing program, such as outlined in Chapter 15, you'll not only have greater success with long-term weight loss, but also have enough energy to run.

3. *If you are at an appropriate weight, practice eating as you did as a child:* Eat when you are hungry, stop when you are content. If you are always hungry and are constantly obsessing about food, you are undoubtedly trying to eat too few calories. Chapter 13 can help you determine an appropriate calorie intake and eating schedule that may differ from your current routine, particularly if you yo-yo between starving and bingeing.

4. *Eat adequate protein.* Research has suggested that amenorrheic runners tend to eat less protein than their regularly menstruating counterparts. Even if you are a vegetarian, remember that you still need adequate protein (see Chapter 7).

5. *Eat at least 20 percent of your calories from fat.* Runners commonly are afraid of eating fat, thinking if they eat fat, they'll get fat. Although excess calories from fat are easily fattening, some fat (20 to 30 percent of total calories) is an appropriate part of a healthy sports diet. (See Chapter 8.)

6. *Maintain a calcium-rich diet to help maintain bone density.* Because you build peak bone density in your teens and early adult years, your goal is to protect against future problems with osteoporosis by including a serving of milk, yogurt and other dairy or calcium-rich foods at each meal in the day. As I mentioned in Chapter 1, a safe target is at least 1,000 milligrams of calcium per day if you are between nineteen and fifty years old, and 1,200 to 1,500 milligrams of calcium per day if you are an amenorrheic or post-menopausal woman or a man over 50 years.

Summary

Food should be one of life's pleasures, a fun part of your running program and a protector of your good health. If you spend too much time thinking about food as being a fattening enemy, I highly recommend you consult with a registered dietitian who specializes in sports nutrition and eating disorders (use the referral network at www.SCANdpg.org). This professional can help you transform your food fears into healthful fueling, so your body can support your running goals with good health, high energy and peaceful feelings towards food and your body.

Turkey Burgers

Ground turkey is a leaner alternative to ground beef. But leaner can sometimes mean "dry and tasteless." This recipe yields a tasty, juicy turkey burger that you'll want to enjoy time and again.

$^1/_2$ cup	(30 g)	uncooked oatmeal
$^1/_2$ cup	(240 ml)	turkey or chicken broth (canned) or milk
1 pound	(450 g)	ground turkey
1 egg or two egg whites		
1 small onion, grated or finely chopped		

Optional: salt, pepper, two dashes of nutmeg

1. In a medium bowl, combine the oatmeal, broth or milk, egg or egg whites, onion and seasonings.
2. Add the ground turkey, mix well, and then shape into 4 patties.
3. Cook over medium heat in a nonstick skillet for about 5 minutes per side.

Yield: 4 patties	
Nutrition Information:	
Total calories:	750
Calories per serving:	190
Carbohydrate:	5 g
Protein:	26 g
Fat:	7 g

Winning Recipe

Chapter 16
Preventing Undesired Weight Loss

If you are thin, and worried about becoming even leaner with added exercise, keep in mind that exercise tends to stimulate the appetite. Yes, a hard run may temporarily "kill" your appetite right after the workout because your body temperature is elevated. But within a few hours when you have cooled down, you will be plenty hungry. The more you exercise, the more you'll want to eat—assuming you make the time to do so.

Here are a few tips to help you boost calories and prevent undesired weight loss.

Six Tips for Boosting Calories

1. Eat consistently.

Have at least three or four hearty meals plus one or two additional snacks daily. Do not skip meals! You may not feel hungry for lunch if you've had a big breakfast, but you should eat regardless. Otherwise, you'll miss out on important calories that you need to accomplish your goal.

"I've always been a bean-pole my whole life; I inherited my Grandma's metabolism. Despite my doubts, running has actually helped me gain weight. I don't know if it's because I gained more muscle mass or if my appetite got better (not that it was ever bad)."

Megan Leahy, Chicago, IL

2. Eat larger portions.

Some runners think they need to buy expensive weight-gain powders. Not the case; standard foods work fine. The only reason commercial powders "work" is because they provide additional calories. For example, one runner religiously drank the recommended three glasses a day of a 300-calorie weight-gain shake; he consumed an extra 900 calories. Although he credited the protein shake for helping him manage his weight, he could have less expensively consumed those calories via supermarket foods.

I suggested that he simply eat larger portions of his standard fare:

* a bigger bowl of cereal
* a larger piece of fruit
* an extra sandwich for lunch
* two potatoes at dinner instead of one
* a taller glass of milk

When he did this, he met his goal of 1,000 extra calories per day and continued to see the desired results.

3. Select higher calorie foods, but not higher fat foods.

Excess fat calories easily convert into body fat that fattens you up rather than bulks up your muscles. The best bet for extra calories is to choose carbohydrate-dense foods that have more calories than an equally enjoyable counterpart (see chart below, How to Boost Your Calories). By reading food labels, you'll be able to make the best choices.

4. Drink lots of juice and low-fat milk.

Beverages are a simple way to increase your calorie intake. Replace part or all of the water you drink with calorie-containing fluids. (You don't need to drink water to get adequate water; juice is 99% water.) Extra juices are not only a great source of calories and fluids but also of carbohydrates to keep your muscles well fueled.

5. Do strength training (push-ups, weightlifting) to stimulate muscular development.

Strength training is essential if you want to bulk up (instead of fatten up). Resistance exercise is the key to muscular development.

6. Be patient.

If you are a scrawny high school or college student, your physique will undoubtedly fill out more easily as you get older. Know that you can be a strong runner by being well fueled and well trained. Your skinny legs may hurt your self-esteem more than your athletic ability.

How to Boost Your Calories

Choose more:	Calories	Amount	Instead of:	Calories	Amount
Cranberry juice	170	8 oz (240 ml)	Orange juice	110	8 ounces
Grape juice	160	8 oz (240 ml)	Grapefruit juice	100	8 ounces
Banana	170	1 large	Apple	130	1 large
Granola	780	1.5 cups (150 g)	Bran flakes	200	1.5 cups (60 g)
Grape-Nuts	660	1.5 cups (175)	Cheerios	160	1.5 cups (45 g)
Corn	140	1 cup (165 g)	Green beans	40	1 cup (120 g)
Carrots	45	1 cup (150 g)	Zucchini	30	1 cup (180 g)
Split pea soup	130	1 cup (240 ml)	Vegetable soup	80	1 cup
Baked beans	260	1 cup (260 g)	Rice	190	1 cup (160 g)

Cheesecake Snackwiches

While standard cheesecake is a nutritional nightmare, this healthier alternative offers the same flavor but with less saturated fat.

These snackwiches are easy to make, and a nice treat for a dessert or afternoon energizer. Graham crackers are considered a whole grain, so this is one tasty way to boost your whole grain intake.

2 graham cracker squares		
1 teaspoon	(5 g)	low fat cream cheese
1 teaspoon	(5 g)	jam
Optional:	sprinkling of cinnamon	

1. Spread one graham cracker with low fat cream cheese.

2. Add the jam; sprinkle with cinnamon, if desired.

3. Top with the second graham cracker, making into a sandwich. Enjoy!

Yield:	1 snackwich
Nutritional Information:	
Total calories:	90 (if you can eat just one!)
Carbohydrate:	16 g
Protein:	2 g
Fat	2 g

143

Afterword

The process of transforming from a non-runner to a dedicated runner is exciting, rewarding and enjoyable when you are properly fueled. (If you are poorly fueled, running will seem like a chore.) Please put into use the food and nutrition tips in this book so you'll be able to enjoy fun and energetic runs. By making wise food choices, you will also invest in your good health for "the long run."

As you transform into an experienced runner, you will learn a lot about your body and your strengths, both mental and physical. You'll learn which foods work and which ones don't. You might even feel a bit nervous as the runs get longer and longer. ("Can I really run that far?") By simply applying the eating advice in this book, you'll be able to create a plan that keeps your body well fueled, appropriately hydrated and prepared to go the distance. You will always win with good nutrition.

Eat well, run well and enjoy miles of smiles!

Nancy Clark

Additional Resources

To find a local sports nutritionist contact:
American Dietetic Association
Tel.: (800) 366-1655
www.eatright.org (click on *Find a Nutrition Professional*)
www.SCANdpg.org (use the referral network)

Newsletters
Tufts University Health & Nutrition Letter
Tel.: (800) 274-7581
http://www.tuftshealthletter.com

University of California at Berkeley Wellness Letter
Tel.: (386) 447-6328
www.berkeleywellness.com

Catalogs for nutrition books and other resources:
Nutrition topics:
Nutrition Counseling and Education Services
Tel.: (888) 545-5653
www.ncescatalog.com

Eating disorders:
Gurze Books
Tel.: (800) 756-7533
www.gurze.net

Fitness and sports nutrition:
Human Kinetics
Tel.: (800) 747-4457
www.humankinetics.com

Meyer & Meyer Sport
www.m-m-sports.com

Recommended Books:

Benardot, Dan. *Advanced Sports Nutrition*. Human Kinetics, 2006.

Clark, Nancy. *Nancy Clark's Sports Nutrition Guidebook,* Fourth Edition. Human Kinetics, 2008.

Clark, Nancy. *The Cyclist's Food Guide: Fueling for the Distance.* www.nancyclarkrd.com, 2005.

Clark, Nancy. *Food Guide for Marathoners.* Meyer & Meyer Sport, 2007

Colberg, Sheri. *The Diabetic Athlete's Handbook.* Human Kinetics, 2008

Duyff, Roberta. The American Dietetic Association's Complete Food and Nutrition Guide. Chronimed Publishing, 2006.

Freedman, Rita. *BodyLove: Learning to Like Our Looks and Ourselves.* Gurze Books, 2002.

Heffner, M. *The Anorexia Workbook: How to accept yourself, heal your suffering & reclaim your life* 2004.

Hirschmann, Jane and Carol Munter. *When Women Stop Hating Their Bodies: Freeing Yourself from Food and Weight Obsession.* Fawcett Books, 1997.

Larsen-Meyer, Enette. *Vegetarian Sports Nutrition.* Human Kinetics, 2006.

LoBue, Andrea and Marsea Marcus. *The Don't Diet, Live-It! Workbook: Healing Food, Weight & Body Issues.* Gurze Books, 1999.

McCabe, Randi and Traci McFarlane. *The Overcoming Bulimia Workbook.* Gurze Books, 2003.

Satter, Ellyn. *Secrets of Feeding a Healthy Family.* Kelcy Press, 1999.

Satter, Ellyn. *Your Overweight Child: Helping Without Harming.* Kelcy Press, 2005

Siegel, Michelle, Judith Brisman and Margot Weinshel. *Surviving an Eating Disorder: Strategies for Families and Friends.* HarperCollins, 1997.

Tribole, Evelyn and Elyse Resch. *Intuitive Eating: A revolutionary program that works.* St. Martins Press, 2003.

For coaches and professionals:

Dunford, Marie Ed. *Sports Nutrition: A Guide for the Professional Working with Active People, Fourth Edition.* American Dietetic Association, 2005.

Internet Resources

Sports and sports nutrition:

Nancy Clark, MS, RD
www.nancyclarkrd.com
Links to nutrition articles and other nutrition sources; information on teaching materials.

Australian Institute of Sport
www.ais.org.au/nutrition
Comprehensive information on physical fitness and nutrition.

Gatorade Sports Science Institute
www.gssiweb.com
Information on endurance sports nutrition.

Sportscience
www.sportsci.org
An interdisciplinary site for research on human physical performance.

WaddleOn.com
www.waddleon.com
An Internet guide to becoming an athlete, whatever your size or shape.

Health and nutrition:

ConsumerLab.com
www.consumerlab.com
Independently tests nutritional supplements and posts the results.

International Food Information Council Foundation
http://ific.org
Geared mostly to health professionals, the site features information on food safety and nutrition.

National Library of Medicine, U.S. Department of Health and Human Services
www.nlm.nih.gov
Free access to abstracts in medical journals.

U.S. Department of Health and Human Services
www.healthfinder.gov
Provides information and lists publications and not-for-profit organizations that produce reliable information.

Eating disorders:

National Eating Disorders Association
www.NationalEatingDisorders.org
Information, resources, and links for eating disorders.

Something Fishy Website on Eating Disorders
www.something-fishy.org
Offers extensive resources and referrals for eating disorders.

Index

Photo & Illustration Credits

Cover design: Jens Vogelsang

Cover photo: imago sportfotodienst GmbH

Inside photos: Fotolia.com

© Giuseppe Porzani:	p. 3, 88-89, 119, 142
© Franz Pfluegl:	p. 3, 6, 7, 43, 69, 70, 130
© Carmen Steiner:	p. 10, 11
© Conny Wöhrlin:	p. 12, 22, 26,
© Laureen Quillet:	p. 13, 48
© Stephan Siedler, (moonrun):	p. 14, 67, 68, 137
© Otmar Smit:	p. 16, 17, 122
© Oliver Hoffmann:	p. 19, 66
© Jens Klingebiel:	p. 28
© fooddesign:	p. 56-57, 70 (bottom)
© Jan Polabinski:	p. 33, 114-115, 57
© Birgit Reitz-Hofmann:	p. 35, 46, 136
© PeJo:	p. 36
© Udo Kroener:	p. 38, 64, 65, 85
© Philip Lange:	p. 39
© Arash Sabbagh:	p. 54, 93
© Liv Friis-larsen:	p. 71
© Elena Elisseeva:	p. 74
© Markus Jesinghaus:	p. 81, 83, 100, 101, 102
© Torsten Schon:	p. 84, 92, 113
© shadowvincent:	p. 30
© seen:	p. 96
© Olivier Delaye:	p. 98, 128, 132
© Olga Lyubkina:	p. 76, 77, 78, 122
© radarreklama:	p. 104, 105
© Simone van den Berg, (Junglefrog Images):	p. 110, 107
© Jesús Arias:	p. 140

About the Author

NANCY CLARK, MS, RD, CSSD

Nancy Clark, MS, RD, CSSD, an internationally known sports nutritionist, is board certified as a specialist in sports dietetics (CSSD). She counsels both competitive athletes and casual exercisers, many of whom are new runners. Her successful private practice is at Healthworks, the premier fitness center in Chestnut Hill MA.

Clark specializes in nutrition for exercise, wellness and the management of eating disorders. Her nutrition advice and photo have been the back of the Wheaties' box! Her clients have included Olympians from a variety of sports, members of the Boston Red Sox, high school athletes and collegiate athletes, including those at Boston College. She has worked with many marathon-training programs and is nutrition consultant to the Leukemia and Lymphoma Society's Team in Training national coaches' education program.

Clark is author of the bestseller *Nancy Clark's Sports Nutrition Guidebook, Fourth Edition* (Human Kinetics, 2008), a book commonly referred to as the "sports nutrition bible." She also writes a monthly nutrition column called *The Athlete's Kitchen*, which appears regularly in over 100 sports and fitness publications, including *New England Runner* Magazine, and is frequently quoted in magazines such as *Runner's World* and *Shape*.

Nancy completed her undergraduate degree in nutrition from Simmons College in Boston, her dietetic internship at Massachusetts General Hospital, and her graduate degree in nutrition with a focus on exercise physiology from Boston University. She is a Fellow of the American Dietetic Association and the American College of Sports Medicine.

Sports and fitness are personal as well as professional interests for Nancy. She is a regular bicycle commuter and runner. She has completed several marathons, bicycled across America and hiked in the Himalayas. She lives in the Boston area with her husband and two teenage children.

For more information, see *www.nancyclarkrd.com*